Bely, Joyce, and Döblin

The Florida James Joyce Series

THE FLORIDA JAMES JOYCE SERIES

Edited by Zack Bowen

The Autobiographical Novel of Co-Consciousness: Goncharov, Woolf, and Joyce, by Galya Diment (1994)

Shaw and Joyce: "The Last Word in Stolentelling," by Martha Fodaski Black (1995)

Bloom's Old Sweet Song: Essays on Joyce and Music, by Zack Bowen (1995)

Reauthorizing Joyce, by Vicki Mahaffey (paperback edition, 1995)

Joyce's Iritis and the Irritated Text: The Dis-lexic Ulysses, by Roy Gottfried (1995)

Joyce, Milton, and the Theory of Influence, by Patrick Colm Hogan (1995)

Jocoserious Joyce: The Fate of Folly in Ulysses, by Robert H. Bell (paperback edition, 1996)

Joyce and Popular Culture, edited by R. B. Kershner (1996)

Bely, Joyce, and Döblin: Peripatetics in the City Novel, by Peter I. Barta (1996)

Bely, Joyce, and Döblin

Peripatetics in the City Novel

Peter I. Barta

UNIVERSITY PRESS OF FLORIDA
Gainesville Tallahassee Tampa Boca Raton
Pensacola Orlando Miami Jacksonville

Copyright 1996 by the Board of Regents of the State of Florida
Printed in the United States of America on acid-free paper
All rights reserved

01 00 99 98 97 96   6 5 4 3 2 1

Library of Congress Cataloging-in-Publication Data

Barta, Peter I.
Bely, Joyce, and Döblin: peripatetics in the city novel / Peter I. Barta
p. cm. — (The Florida James Joyce series)
Includes bibliographical references (p.) and index.
ISBN 0-8130-1450-6 (cloth: alk. paper)
1. Joyce, James, 1882–1941. Ulysses. 2. Literature, Comparative—English and European. 3. Literature, Comparative—European and English. 4. Bely, Andrey, 1880–1934. Petersburg. 5. Saint Petersburg (Russia)—In literature. 6. Döblin, Alfred, 1878–1957. Berlin Alexanderplatz. 7. Berlin (Germany)—In literature. 8. City and town life in literature. 9. Cities and towns in literature. 10. Dublin (Ireland)—In literature. 11. Modernism (Literature). 12. Walking in literature. I. Title. II. Series.
PR6019.O9U624 1996
809.3'9321732—dc20   96-142

Cover: Gustave Caillebotte, *Paris Street, Rainy Day* (1876–77). Courtesy of the Art Institute of Chicago, Charles H. and Mary F. S. Worcester Collection.

The University Press of Florida is the scholarly publishing agency for the State University System of Florida, comprised of Florida A & M University, Florida Atlantic University, Florida International University, Florida State University, University of Central Florida, University of Florida, University of North Florida, University of South Florida, and University of West Florida.

University Press of Florida
15 Northwest 15th Street
Gainesville, FL 32611

To P. S. L., my Mother and Father,
K. R., and P. P.

". . . he continued to wander up and down day after day as if he really sought someone that eluded him"

JAMES JOYCE

Contents

Foreword, by Zack Bowen   xi

Preface   xiii

1. The Emergence of the Modernist City Novel and Its Peripatetic Hero   1
2. Knights and Unicorns: The Walkers of *Petersburg*   19
3. *Ulysses:* The City of the Wandering Aengus and the Wandering Jew   47
4. Walking in the Shadow of Death: *Berlin Alexanderplatz*   76

Conclusion   99

Notes   103

Bibliography   107

Index   119

Foreword

The Florida James Joyce Series is dedicated to pursuing roads that form broader links with traditional and sometimes less traditional literary study. Peter Barta's book develops one of these links. Barta juxtaposes *Petersburg, Ulysses,* and *Berlin Alexanderplatz,* as modernist novels viewed principally through the eyes of character-observers who wander about in cities in which they play only marginalized social roles. Not mere members of a faceless crowd, but highly individualized characters, these walker-observers in their respective urban metropolises provide the basis for Barta's acute comparative analysis of three discrete texts as well as a tripartite conceptual entity, the city novel. The method allows for analytic approaches along various lines, but always within the context of the overall scheme. The extensive cross-referencing among the three novels should provide a new frame of reference for Joyceans unfamiliar with Bely and Döblin.

Zack Bowen
Series Editor

Preface

This book is about walking in the modernist European novel. The activity of rambling about the city is more than a literary theme; undoubtedly, it is important to see who walks, where, and why, but in addition, wandering creates a city text that is determined by its peripatetic narrative. The etymology of the term "peripatetic" illuminates some important aspects of the modernist city novel. The Peripatetic scholars walked about the Peripatos, the covered grounds of the school Aristotle established in Athens in 335–34 B.C.E. Classical scholars today argue that the notion that prominent philosophers and writers in ancient Greece taught their pupils while walking may be exaggerated. Nevertheless, the writings of the "Peripatetics" frequently reveal an interest in the world around them rather than in primarily abstract, moral argumentation. Theophrastus, Aristotle's successor, was an empiricist who strongly preferred sensory observations to speculative synthesis. In his *Characters*, thirty types are sketched in an emphatically lifelike fashion. Subsequent, often biographical literature of the Peripatos by such lesser authors as Aristoxenus and Phaenias of Erasos is also informed by an interest in concrete examples, anecdotes, and legends. The combination of rambling, thinking, observing, and talking creates a "peripatetic" perspective, a manner of facing the world and oneself, that is germane to the subject of this book: how a text of walking produces the idiosyncratic features of the modernist European city novel.

Andrei Bely's *Petersburg*, James Joyce's *Ulysses*, and Alfred Döblin's *Berlin Alexanderplatz* are the most prominent modernist city novels in European literature. They share analogous textual features and thus comprise a subgenre. Walking is a theme of central significance in each novel; it accounts for the ever-present multiple perspective of the many-voiced text. The slow, strolling movement about the city in the plot produces a uniquely close tie between the central human characters and their urban environment; together, city and walker serve as these novels' protagonists. The narrative voice is unstable in each text because of the constant change of scenery, storytellers, characters, and milieux. The coming chapters will examine the forces that motivate wandering about the three textual capitals, St. Petersburg, Dublin, and Berlin; we will pay special attention to how the rambling narrative juxtaposes details of the city with details of the characters' mental wanderings to create the many-colored, fragmented surface of the modernist novel.

The first chapter will discuss the generic background of the modernist city novel. It begins with a brief survey of urban literature of the last three hundred years, in order to trace the history of narrative accounts of walkers in cities. When texts adopt the viewpoint of the literary character who has come to be known as the "flâneur," classic realist order and harmony in the text is violated. As the flâneur gradually merges with the "badaud" of the capitalist city, a collage of details appears and the centered viewpoint is confused by the release of the subconscious. The result is a new type of novel that is singularly well suited to create a vivid literary image of the big city.

Subsequent chapters will analyze each of the three novels as a text of urban walking. Events in Bely's *Petersburg* take place during the revolution of October 1905 in the Russian capital. Apollon Apollonovich Ableukhov, the prominent statesman, is the target of an assassination attempt, masterminded and unsuccessfully carried out by two revolutionaries and his own son, Nikolai Apollonovich, a confused and unhappy student. Joyce's *Ulysses* carefully catalogues events involving and surrounding Stephen Dedalus and Leopold and Molly Bloom in Dublin on 16 June 1904. The novel's "epic totality" features a modernist reworking of *The Odyssey*; a sense of universality is achieved by mapping both the conscious and subconscious realms of the mind in addition to creating the most sensitively drawn image of any city in literature. Döblin's *Berlin Alexanderplatz* follows the story of Franz Biberkopf, a petty criminal in Berlin in the 1920s, who craves in vain the blessings of bourgeois "decency." Döblin projects a broad canvas of people's lives in the Eastern part of the city that is home to the protagonist. Seemingly the three plots have little in common, but importantly, in each novel the walkers wander about—often without a clear purpose—because they feel they are dispossessed. Finding little comfort in the surroundings of home and family, they look for an alternative center of meaning. They expect to find this behind the many faces of the city, which resembles the home; it, too, is "surrounded," since it is supposed to protect civilized values behind its by now metaphorical walls. Walkers roam the city and "read" it as a collection of randomly juxtaposed signs; they are driven by desire to locate a source of meaning behind crowds, buildings, and glittering lights. However, the center is forever hidden among the details; it inevitably disappears in the many-voiced narrative.

The modern text defies the conventional boundaries imposed by plot, character, three-dimensional space, and historical time. The city-text, a maze without a center, dispossesses its sons and daughters, but in spite of this, they do not lose hope and the desire to come to terms with their environment. Yet the city does not change nor do characters come to a better understanding of it. Their personal displacement in the world is rooted in their inability to turn the city into a protective place, the metaphorical "home," without which human well-being is inconceivable. By necessity, each text fails to resolve the conflicts responsible for the restless peregrinations about the metropolis.

I would like to express my sense of gratitude, first and foremost, to the late Professor Bernard Benstock for his interest in my work on Joyce and the city novel. In writing the book, I found his many ideas invaluable. I am grateful to David H. J. Larmour for his numerous perceptive suggestions regarding both content and form and for reading attentively several drafts of the manuscript. I would like to thank Paul G. Ratcliffe for helping me with the corrections of the final draft and for making useful comments in matters of style and presentation. Thanks to successive honorary visiting fellowships at the School of Slavonic and East European Studies of the University of London, I was able to use the school's outstanding library and reference services. Much of the research was done in the British Library and at the library of the University of Illinois at Champaign-Urbana. I also enjoyed the benefits of being a research associate at the Russian and East European Center of the University of Illinois at Champaign-Urbana on two occasions while completing work on the project. I am grateful to Angela Gammon and to Richard Nice for their technical assistance. Finally, I would like to acknowledge the following colleagues and former teachers from whom I received many useful suggestions: Galya Diment, Walter Höllerer, James Hurt, François Jost, Sidney Monas, and Lena Szilard.

CHAPTER I

The Emergence of the Modernist City Novel and Its Peripatetic Hero

Cities are as old as the term "civilization." Even superficial etymological probes will point to the relationship between the two words: "civitas" is the Latin equivalent of the Greek "polis," and each means both "community" and "city." Their derivatives, such as the words "civilization" and "politics," appear in most European languages, suggesting that those building cities intend to preserve, or bring about, human communities whose conduct is governed by laws. In the *Politics*, according to Aristotle's basic premise, the "idiotes"—the private man—is also "politikos"—naturally disposed to live in cities. In his book, *The City in History*, Lewis Mumford reasserts that the city "is a place designed to offer the highest facilities for significant conversation" (1961, 157). Yet dissatisfaction with urban life has always accompanied the enthusiasm. The phenomenon of "alienation"—over-used as it may be by critics today—was already present in classical portrayals of the city. In Euripides' play, *The Bacchae*, Pentheus surrounds his urban civilization with walls but secretly yearns for the very force lacking in his realm, against which he fortifies his city: the unrestraint and libidinal freedom that the Dionysian countryside offers (Barta 1991–92). In Juvenal's third *Satire*, Rome's vileness and mass society threaten to destroy Umbricius and so he leaves the capital, although Juvenal does not: his love-hate relationship with the city keeps him there.

Duality surrounds the city's image in Judeo-Christian culture too. The "City of God"—desirable as it may be—receives a far less detailed description than the "City of Man"—immoral and flawed as it is. "Babylon the Great, the mother of harlots" is a sharper and more specific image in the book of Revelation than the vaguely-depicted "New Jerusalem." Of course, life in real cities has always resembled the image the Bible produces of Babylon rather than Augustine's fictional "City of God." Literary descriptions of the latter are vaguely delineated and few. In Chaucer's *Canterbury Tales* we learn little about the "good" city: Canterbury—very impressive in the red rays of the setting sun—remains obscure, whereas the "bad" cities in many pilgrims' tales are described with great specificity. Likewise, in Dante's *Divine Comedy*, the longest and finest part of the epic is not about Paradise in the sky or Purgatory on a lonely island but about Hell, a city of grief, surrounded by walls like the actual medieval cities that his readers recognized all too well.

Favorable and hostile literary accounts tend to fuse increasingly as medieval towns turn into big cities. Until the seventeenth century, urban centers had a relatively structured design with a predictable prevailing order: a castle or major churches, surrounded by living quarters, dominated the center. Richer people would live closer to, and the poorer ones further away from, the middle of the town. In many European capital cities, the seventeenth, eighteenth, and early nineteenth centuries witnessed the disintegration of this traditional pattern of urban development; a much larger and much less tidy entity arises. Many writers have a love-hate relationship with their city, whose sudden growth can threaten their well-being even as it provides a hitherto unknown form of intellectual stimulation. Wordsworth, despite being the author of *The Prelude*, with its strongly anti-urban ideas, nevertheless cannot suppress his joy as he beholds London, the location of his walk, in the poem "Upon Westminster Bridge":

> Earth has not anything to show more fair:
> Dull would he be of soul who could pass by
> A sight so touching in its majesty:
> This City now doth, like a garment, wear
> The beauty of the morning; silent, bare,
> Ships, towers, domes, theatres, and temples lie
> Open unto the fields, and to the sky;
> All bright and glittering in the smokeless air.
> Never did sun more beautifully steep
> In his first splendour, valley, rock, or hill;
> Ne'er saw I, never felt, a calm so deep!
> The river glideth at his own sweet will:
> Dear God! the very houses seem asleep;
> And all that mighty heart is lying still!

Likewise, the Dickens of *Little Dorrit* and *Bleak House* — uncovering the negative aspects of city life — is distressed when personally removed from the London streets. We read in his letter from Switzerland: "I can't express how much I want these [streets]. It seems as if they supplied something to my brain, which I cannot bear, when busy, to lose" (Dickens 1965, 4:162).

Because of its social and economic impact, the nineteenth-century city infiltrates individual lives even in the heart of the country, far away from urban centers. The city affects forever the lives of characters whom it attracts from the country or those who come into contact with its envoys in the village. Failed expectations and destruction await "poor Evgeny" in Pushkin's "Bronze Horseman," a suburban resident of the city and, by all probability, a man of rural origin. His pursuit of modest personal goals is thwarted by a flood—a natural disaster—in a city built for commercial and strategic advantages in geographically highly unsuitable terrain. Here, as in other large and successful European cities, the prosperous and influential social classes view happiness increasingly in economic rather than spiritual terms (Robinson 1989, 6). Stendhal's Julien Sorel in *The Red and the Black* forsakes his country innocence for Paris only to fail in his ambitious attempt at social advancement. Pushkin's Onegin—a bored Petersburg dandy in search of new excitements—carries the ways of the "experienced" city to the "innocent" village and disrupts happy lives there. A similar outcome occurs when Lermontov's embittered "superfluous man" in *A Hero of Our Time*—typifying urban sophistication, egotism, and a purposeless existence—interferes in the lives of people of non-urban societies. Turgenev's frustrated intellectual arrives at the country home of the provincial gentry, having obtained his formative experiences alongside his academic training in the city. Pavel Aleksandrovich in the story "Faust" or the protagonist of *Rudin* disrupt rural tranquility: they make the heroine fall in love with them by parading as representatives of an educated, enlightened, and superior urban society.

In order to account for the changing quality of life in the expanding city, we need to consider the physical realities in addition to the psychological ones. Far-reaching as its influence may be, the nineteenth-century metropolis is anything but unified: the physical division between the affluent and the impoverished becomes broader than ever. Disraeli's "two nations"—signifying the split between the rich and the poor in the Britain of 1845—appear in cities in an architecturally marked way: the meandering medieval streets disappear, having for many centuries offered a potentially cramped and unhealthy, nevertheless integral, form of urban life to their dwellers, to be replaced by broad avenues separating wealth from poverty (Clark 1985, 58). In big European cities, the squalor of small hovels disguises itself behind the facade of the new tenement houses. Furthermore, the big, unattractive, uniform blocks of working-class flats comprise the slums of the periphery where better-off people have no reason to go. The major avenues, built to accommodate large-scale traffic and well-appointed shops with ostentatious windows subdivide cities into districts that typify the socioeconomic features of the people populating them. St. Petersburg—a creation of the eighteenth century—already reflects this principle of urban planning. The new "urban morphology" signified by such thoroughfares as the Strand, Piccadilly, Oxford Street, or Regent Street, is fully in place in London by the middle of the eighteenth century (Brand 1991, 39). The long avenues imposed on nineteenth-century Paris by Baron Haussmann appear in many other prominent European cities too. The boulevards make the city less unified, and just as they offer protection to the newly affluent bourgeois walker, they isolate and expose poverty. This is clearly apparent in the topography of the city in Gogol's "Overcoat." As Akaky Akakievich is walking away from the well-lit avenue, the streets are becoming dark and desolate. The police are too busy looking after the safety of the prosperous crowd on the boulevard, and the thieves have every opportunity to dispossess their vulnerable victim. Akaky Akakievich is unsure where he is: because of its size and diversity, the city is now no longer a fully knowable place. As the commercial city of the eighteenth century turns into the industrial city of the nineteenth century, heralding the twentieth-century world city (Lehan 1986, 99), it ceases to be possible to survey it with the naked eye. When the metropolis appears in the second half of the nineteenth century, its edges extend too far into the country to be seen without a telescope even from such high points as London's Highgate or Paris' Montmartre (Girouard 1985, 343).

Two prominent traditions evolved in literary renderings of the urban experience after 1666, the year of the fire that destroyed much of medieval London, marking the beginnings of the modern European city. In the more significant of the two traditions, the urban theme offers background to the plot and the characters and establishes the *couleur locale*. Many eighteenth- and nineteenth-century novels whose scenery is the city belong to this category. Dickens' London characters, Balzac's Parisians, and Tolstoy's pronouncedly different Moscow and Petersburg heroes typify, and are inseparable from, their city.[1] In fiction set in St. Petersburg the city often arises as a mythical construction and creates its own *homo peterburgiensis*. Variants of the "Petersburg text," such as Pushkin's "Queen of Spades," Gogol's "Portrait" and "Overcoat," Dostoevsky's *Poor People*, *White Nights*, and *Crime and Punishment* all include characters who, like the plots they enact, characterize the Russian capital.

The other type of literary depiction of the city has attracted less interest. Here, the figure of the city itself is in the foreground of the text; plot and character are secondary or do not play any role at all. While all the famous eighteenth- and nineteenth-century novels set in cities fit into the first category, this alternative type of urban literature appeared in such shorter prose forms as diaries, essays, and sketches. Instead of elaborately portrayed protagonists, the central figure tends to be a wandering observer-narrator whose personality and circumstances remain outside the text's focus and whose primary significance lies in his consciousness, which produces an impression of the city. In accounts of this type, the city resembles the carnival. Passers-by in the streets and squares may suddenly be confronted by unexpected and disconcerting aspects of life. The narrative of strolling captures and juxtaposes incongruous details of the cityscape and transforms them into elements of a text. This process saves both the city and its observer from the passage of time, death, and oblivion (Brand 1989, 31).

Perhaps for this reason, great disasters, threatening entire urban populations, often provide the opportunity to present the city in journalistic sketches that capture the urban spectacle. Entries on the Great Fire of London in Pepys' *Diaries* or Heine's travel notes about a Paris plagued by cholera offer something different from the mere scenery of a structured story; instead, the city here *is* the story.[2]

> Wherever one looked in the streets, there he saw funerals, or sadder still, hearses with no one following. But as there were not hearses sufficient, all kinds of vehicles were used, which, when covered with black stuffs, looked very strange. Even these were at last wanting, and I saw coffins carried in hackney-coaches. It was most disagreeable to see the great furniture-wagons which were used for "moving" now moving about as dead men's omnibuses, or omnibus mortuis, going from house to house for fares and carrying them by dozens to the field of rest. (Heine 1983, 182–83)

Heine's vignettes draw upon sights that the casual wandering observer captures; he is not preoccupied by any urgent personal business and has plenty of time. The walker gathering details, wandering around out of curiosity, driven by a desire to learn and understand, is the flâneur. In order to keep control over the constantly changing, unstable mess of the city, the flâneur's account domesticates the spectacle by turning it into the chatty text of the feuilleton (Brand 1991, 24).

The flâneur emerges simultaneously with the growth of the city in the late seventeenth century and gains more prominence by the nineteenth century. The term "flâneur" is French: Walter Benjamin, who studied the figure perhaps the most extensively, places its origin in the Paris magazines of the 1830s. This may certainly hold true for the genesis of the term but less so for the social-literary type it signifies. Benjamin failed to take into consideration the semiotic importance of the urban arcade and the "culture of the spectacle" in late-sixteenth- and seventeenth-century London, not to mention the well-developed literary journalism of the English capital by the eighteenth century (Brand 1991, 6–7, 14).

The phenomenon of "flânerie" was obviously quite widespread in nineteenth-century urban Europe; many European cultures adopted the term. In German, both the verb "flanieren" and the noun "Flâneur" entered the written and the conversational language; in Russian, both the noun "flanyor" and the verb "flanirovat" exist, but are not commonly used. According to Ozhegov's dictionary, the activity is performed when one wanders about without anything to do. In English, the term does not enjoy common currency. However, the titles of such eighteenth-century English journals as Addison and Steele's *Spectator* or Dr. Johnson's *Rambler* suggest the kind of leisurely introspection and commentary about social and moral matters in an increasingly urbanized society that are identical with the continental flâneur's. The urban journalism of Addison and Steele brings together features of sixteenth-century survey books, Theophrastian character books, and the viewpoint of the city's bawdy, "carnivalesque spectator" (Brand 1991, 31–33). The description we read in an issue of *The Spectator* defines the flâneur:

> I have passed my latter years in this city, where I am frequently seen in most public places, though there are not above half a dozen of my select friends that know me. . . ; I have been taken for a merchant upon the Exchange for above these ten years, and sometimes pass for a Jew in the assembly of stock-jobbers at Jonathan's. In short, wherever I see a cluster of people, I always mix with them, though I never open my lips. . . . Thus I live in the world rather as a Spectator of mankind. . . . I have acted in all the parts of my life as a looker-on. (Addison and Steele, 1832, 1:17–18)

The passage implies that the "spectator" wishes to retain his anonymity. Thus, he fills his essay with urban details gathered with sensitivity and attentiveness and, purportedly, without taking sides.

In the nineteenth century, the flâneur is still a wealthy gentleman with plenty of time on his hands. Fewer people of leisure walk about the streets than in eighteenth-century London; the big European city is now buzzing with opportunities and the excitement of self-advancement. The reason that the flâneur does not participate in commercial, bureaucratic, or industrial ventures is that he—an increasingly anachronistic figure by now—no longer feels at home in a more and more materialistic age. The narrator in Gogol's "Nevsky Prospect" is such a figure. While he, as narrator, remains in the background of the sketch, we surmise from his comments and tone that he is well-educated and has plenty of free time to observe Nevsky Prospect from dawn to nightfall. He is condescending about the pretensions and vulgarity of the city's new, commercially minded middle classes. He is clearly not one of them, but he does not belong to the world of the Petersburg bureaucracy either. His interest in Nevsky Prospect is not accidental; it is pointed out emphatically that the ministries and government offices are *not* on Nevsky Prospect. He comments: "It is as if the people one meets on the Nevsky Prospect are not such egoists as those one meets in the Morskaya, the Gorochovaya, the Liteynaya, the Meshchanskaya and other streets, where greed, avarice and want are reflected from every coach and droshky, fast or slow" (Gogol 1945, 124). While in this city of appearances, Gogol's reader is well advised not to disregard the phrase "as if" in the sentence, it is nevertheless one of the few certainties of the story that Nevsky Prospect, egotistical or not, offers more of a spectacle than it is an area for business. "It is the only place in all Petersburg to which people do not go because they must, to which they are not driven by some private need or business interest" (Gogol 1945, 124), says the narrator endowed with the perspective of the flâneur. While he dons the mask of a detached observer he complements his ironical tone with genuine compassion. The many signs of human suffering and loneliness he witnesses in the big, impersonal capital sadden him. Although he cannot effect any changes in the urban world, he can at least exercise some control by turning experience into textual account. Aloofness and sympathy smoothly coexist in "Nevsky Prospect":

> I do not like bodies or dead men and I always find it unpleasant when a long funeral procession crosses my path and I see an old soldier, wearing some sort of cloak, taking snuff with his left hand, because his right is occupied with the torch. I am always annoyed by the sight of a rich catafalque and a velvet coffin, but my annoyance is mixed with sadness when I see drawn on a cart the red coffin of a poor man, uncovered and with only some beggar woman, encountered by chance at the cross roads and having nothing else to do, dragging after it. (Gogol 1945, 144–45)

The same duality of perspective is apparent in the juxtaposition of the stories of the artist Piskarev and of Lieutenant Pirogov. The unity between the two different stories rests in the place, Nevsky Prospect, where the two accidental acquaintances meet briefly and the observant narrator-flâneur follows them.

Another type of observing gentleman in the city opts to see but not to be seen. He may prefer to watch the city from a height, isolated above everything else. In an unsigned essay in *The London Magazine* in August 1822, entitled "The Tea Garden," the storyteller, by his own admission a man "vegetating for the most part in the solitude of the study" is driven out of doors by the hot weather. He walks up to the top of Primrose Hill to see London: "The bird's eye view of it which was before me diminished its aggregate effects. The inhabitants were to me as ants in their little cells, and I was a giant Brobdingnag contemplating them." Referring to himself as a "mere bookworm" in isolation, he suggests that he is different from the mainstream of busy city people, an "intellectual" among the moneymakers. However, people in the London "bookworm's" environment do not regard his lifestyle as fashionable; hence the defensive tone of the passage. The distance of the observer from the observed emphasizes the sense of separation from the hustle and bustle of the city. Furthermore, the narrator's self-analogy to a Brobdingnagian, a subject in the kingdom of giants in Swift's *Gulliver's Travels*, suggests in rather strong terms that the isolated narrator feels different and superior. He is above while the crowd is below; he can see them all while they cannot even see themselves. In the description of the cholera-ridden city that was discussed before, Heine expresses far more sympathy towards the citizen, but the perspective is the same as in "The Tea Garden": "I hastened to the *highest hill* of the cemetery, whence one may see the city spread out in all its beauty. The sun was setting; its last rays seemed to bid me a sad good-bye. . . ; and I wept bitterly over the unhappy city" (Heine 1983, 185; my emphasis). Here, again, the observer stands separated from the city: he, the outsider, is healthy while the crowd below is not; he is alive and the citizens are dead.

In less tragic accounts, as the flâneur unhurriedly wanders about and perceives himself somewhat of an outsider, he is still a respectable citizen. Walter Benjamin, the author of *Passagenwerk*—an unfinished masterpiece on flânerie—writes that "around the 1840s it was fashionable to take turtles for a walk in the arcades" (Benjamin 1972, 5:532). The irony in the image suggests that the walking gentlemen were very comfortable, strolling about extremely slowly. Furthermore, the activity was "fashionable": the flâneur cannot have been an unusual sight and he also must have enjoyed enough prestige to create a vogue. As a worthy person of independent means, the flâneur carries his own aura around with dignity wherever he goes, like the turtle, which carries its "house" everywhere.

Alternatively, the flâneur may choose isolation by avoiding the street altogether and contemplate other people's behavior from a sedentary position inside; he may prefer to sit behind a window and drink in the crowd with his eyes as in the first part of Poe's story, "The Man of the Crowd." Unknown to all as an American in London, the narrator has avoided the streets for some time because of an illness. He can observe the street from his viewing position beside the window in a restaurant. Here again, he enjoys superiority over the objects of his vision thanks to his position, which allows him to survey the crowd from inside. He proceeds to "read" the crowd as one reads the paper. Frequently a similarly isolated figure does the narrating in Dickens' *Sketches by Boz*, as, for example, in "Hackney-Coach Stands." Detached, he sits behind a window looking at the events of the street below, contemplating how the "memories" of hackney coaches may complement the stories of people's lives, about which he, the flâneur, can only make guesses.

In all the examples above, the observers of the city streets choose isolation. However, gradually, isolation becomes the only alternative rather than a matter of choice for many artists in the nineteenth century. An unprecedented explosion of scientific advances in the fields of transportation, communication, and industrial technology affects all levels of the dramatically rising populations of London, Paris, New York, St. Petersburg, and Berlin. Materialistic, purpose-oriented societies of the age make many a vulnerable or artistically sensitive person feel unwanted and unnecessary; sensibility comes to be regarded as an extravagant and unproductive luxury. Symbolist literature and postimpressionistic painting depict the inward turning of the artist, who no longer seems willing to accommodate the taste of the wealthy consumers of literature and the arts; rather than the easily comprehensible "realistic" reflection of society, the new object of art becomes the response that the inner world offers to the stimuli of the outer world. The flâneur, whose perspective is particularly prone to this kind of expression, may rejoice in his freedom but the figure turns from outsider into outcast and becomes marginal in city society. We read in "Crowds," one of the stories in Baudelaire's *Paris Spleen*: "It is not given to every man to take a bath of multitude: enjoying a crowd is an art; and only he can relish a debauch of vitality at the expense of the human species, on whom, in his cradle, a fairy has bestowed the love of masks and masquerading, the hate of the home and the passion for roaming" (Baudelaire 1947, 16). Isolation is no longer his choice but an unavoidable consequence of the dominance of a value system whose rules are set exclusively by the interests of the business world. The walker-observer now explicitly acknowledges his stance *against* the bourgeois majority—the "human species"—and the joyously peripatetic perspective identifies with those who "hate home" and have a "passion for roaming." Benjamin comments in *Charles Baudelaire: A Lyric Poet in the Era of High Capitalism:* "To the flâneur the shiny signs of business are at least as good as a wall ornament or oil painting is to a bourgeois in his salon. The walls are the desk against which he presses his notebooks; newsstands are his libraries" (Benjamin 1973, 37).

As an outsider both to the bourgeois home and to the bourgeois business, the flâneur appropriates the public space of the street and converts it into his own intimate world. To him advertisements become decoration; he undermines the system as he merely browses but does not buy. This is his reaction to the city that has marginalized him. Peripheral in the city, the flâneur finds a *raison d'être* in observation: lack of a purposeful role to perform in society appears as a virtue rather than a vice to him. The flâneur will be preoccupied by phenomena that other people — rushing about their business — are likely to miss.

Gradually, however, the activity of dawdling about completely loses any semblance of respectability, and the walker as a literal "man of the crowd" can lose his standing as an individual. Benjamin distinguishes between the flâneur and a new, nineteenth-century type, the "badaud": "The flâneur is always in full possession of his individuality; the individuality of the badaud, however, disappears: he is no individual any more but part of the public, of the mass" (Benjamin 1973, 74–75). The badaud lacks the sheltering intimate space to which the flâneur can return from his pleasurable walks. The badaud draws on the possibilities of the street: the crowds can hide him and offer him some kind of companionship. Loafing about is an existential need for him rather than a source of pleasure. The world of prostitution and crime surrounds him, whereas the flâneur occupies a far more dignified place in urban society.

The first literary encounter between the flâneur and the badaud occurs in the second part of Poe's "Man of the Crowd." Having fancied himself as the "reader" of the crowd with the power to impose order on it, the narrator departs from the coffeehouse and follows a mysterious old man for twenty-four hours without learning anything about him. The old man functions in the city not as an individual but as one of the mass. He remains incomprehensible to his pursuer; the narrator — a flâneur — is forced to realize that his intellectual superiority and his power of imposing control over the urban spectacle before his eyes rest on shaky ground.

Both the flâneur and the badaud appear in Dostoevsky's *Crime and Punishment*. The protagonist, Raskolnikov, uses the city's streets as a disguise: before and after committing the double murder, he attempts to become one with the crowd so as not to be noticed, thereby displaying certain features of the badaud. At one point, shortly after committing the crime, Raskolnikov feverishly walks to the Hay Market where he listens to an organ-grinder. Next to him stands "a man no longer young, who had been standing beside him listening to the organ-grinder and who looked like a flâneur" (Dostoevsky 1980, 160). Raskolnikov engages him in conversation, but his appearance and eccentric, impassioned speech frighten the "flâncur," a "gentleman" (160), who refuses to treat him as an individual but instead regards his comments as an affront from the crude mass; he quickly crosses over to the other side of the street. Although both of them loaf about Hay Market without a definite purpose, the marked socioeconomic distance prevents successful communication between the two men.

Walter Benjamin's own experience suggests that being a walker of the city can be an unpleasant result of modern urban deprivation and homelessness. Benjamin writes in a letter that the houses along the street "do not seem to be made to be lived in, but are like stone sets for people to walk between." Thomas Hardy comments that "as the crowd goes denser, it loses its character as an aggregate of countless units, and becomes an organic whole, a molluscous, black creature having nothing in common with humanity" (F. E. Hardy 1928, 179). Dostoevsky also accounts for the impact of a dehumanized city on the human subject. The narrating protagonist of *White Nights* has no alternative to spending the hot summer in Petersburg. He has no acquaintances other than the complete strangers whom he keeps seeing on his walks. Without any human companions, he establishes "relationships" with the city houses along his way: these houses seem to "talk" to him and "know" him.

The metropolitan walker's sense of not belonging bears external marks too. Thomas Hardy writes: "Each individual is conscious of himself but nobody is conscious of themselves collectively, except perhaps some poor gaper who stares round with a half-idiotic aspect" (F. E. Hardy 1928, 71). Such individuals in Dostoevsky's Petersburg are referred to as "dreamers." As they walk about the streets of Petersburg, they seem ridiculous to people hurrying about, conscious only of their most immediate needs and interests and essentially unconcerned with the world around them and their place in it. Dostoevsky defines the "Petersburg dreamer" in *Petersburg News* in 1847 as follows:

> Are there many Russians who have discovered what their real activity is? . . . It is then . . . what is known as dreaminess that arises in characters who are eager for activity. And do you know what a Petersburg dreamer is, gentlemen? . . . In the streets he walks, with a drooping head, paying little atten-

tion to his surroundings, . . . but if he does notice something, even the most ordinary trifle, the most insignificant fact assumes the most fantastic colouring in his mind. Indeed, his mind seems attuned to perceive the fantastic elements in everything. . . . These gentlemen are no good at all in the civil service, though they sometimes get jobs. (cited from Berman 1982, 173)

Unlike Benjamin's flâneurs, dreamers spend a great deal of time indoors. Whereas in *Passagenwerk* the turtle is the flâneur's walking companion, in *White Nights* the main character, himself like a tortoise, hides away from the world in his room. When he comes out,

[I]t is not with indifference that he looks at the sunset which is slowly fading on the cold Petersburg sky. . . . Look! he is thinking of something. Of dinner perhaps? Or how he is going to spend the evening? What is he looking at like that? At the gentleman of the solidly prosperous exterior who is bowing so picturesquely to the lady who drives past in a splendid carriage drawn by a pair of mettlesome horses? No, Nastenka, what do all those trivial things matter to him now? He is rich beyond compare with his own individual life; he has become rich in the twinkling of an eye. . . . Now he hardly notices the road on which every other time every trivial detail would have attracted his attention. . . . Frowning with vexation, he walks on, scarcely aware of the passers-by who smile as they look at him and turn round to follow him with their eyes. (Dostoevsky 1968, 164–65)

In *Crime and Punishment,* Svidrigailov explains to Raskolnikov why Petersburg in particular attracts such "dreamers" to its streets. His words will reverberate throughout Andrei Bely's *Petersburg:* "[L]ots of people in Petersburg go around talking to themselves. It's a city of the half insane. . . . Not many places bring to bear such gloomy, harsh, and strange influences on the spirit of man as Petersburg. Just think of the climate alone! And it's the administrative center of all Russia, so its character is imprinted on everything!" (Dostoevsky 1980, 450) The "half insane," "the poor gaper," the "dreamer" are the only ones in the busy crowd who transcend the *hic et nunc,* who are capable of reverie. As they wander about, they observe physical phenomena that set them off on a connotative-associative mental walk. This condition makes these city wanderers particularly liable to rise above spatial and temporal boundaries. In the poetry of the fin de siècle and the beginning of the twentieth century, as well as in Rilke's lyrical prose work, *The Notebooks of Malte Laurids Brigge,* the walker-protagonist of the street completely internalizes the city impressions;

places of the present melt with places of the past and the only reality is the one inside the soul.

At the beginning of the twentieth century, when many of the best writers and artists no longer feel that they can advance awareness of life in traditional, representational, sequential-causal terms, the type of the randomly observing, marginal walker gains prominence in prose fiction about the big city. Inherited narrative traditions now prove incapable of imaging the metropolis adequately: in most forms of art the semblance of "order" virtually disappears in accounts of the rapid and hitherto unprecedented expansion of the urban population and territorial growth. As the arts cannot avail themselves of a unified viewpoint of the world any more, art becomes essentially "modern." Subjective perception and inner response offer more truthful accounts than the stale, photographic reflection of the rationalizing tendencies of artistic positivism. Mimesis, Aristotelian logic, Euclidean geometry, and Newtonian physics appear inadequate for coming to terms with the world around (Spears 1970, 61). A new style and a different type of narrative, suitable for the textual re-creation of rapid multiple perspectives, replace the worn-out discourse of classic realism. The literary collage, like the montage in the new genre, the film, provides a sharp contrast with the artificial tidiness of conventional nineteenth-century art (Minden 1985, 113).

The urban literature of the time welcomes precisely the glimpses afforded by the "illogical" sequence of the walker's perception. Before we move on to the specific subject of this book, how the peripatetic perspective accounts for the specific features of the modernist city novel, let us examine briefly how the treatment of the city's walker in modernist poetry differs from that in prose. In symbolist and expressionist poetry (and in poetic prose of the type of Rilke's *Notebooks of Malte Laurids Brigge*), it is usually the case that one, often semi- or fully autobiographical, persona wanders about the city and his or her voice dominates. We hear many voices in T. S. Eliot's long poem, "The Waste Land," and yet the image of the city arises from a single viewpoint. In Eliot's shorter poems about the city, as in the verses of the prominent Russian symbolist, Aleksandr Blok, the city projects the poet's inner, psychic state. In such poems by Blok as "Deception" ("Obman," 1904) or "Hymn" ("Gimn," 1904), the persona observes the milieu of the city but pays little or no attention to the metonymic relationship between the details that comprise the scene and create the atmosphere. He concerns himself with a hidden meaning centered in the heavily symbol-laden environment (Masing-Delic 1973, 90). The fragments that characterize symbolist and expressionist city poetry symbolize a transcendental reality. The urban imagery stands for any or all big cities rather than a particular one. In Blok's poem "They Ascended from the Darkness of the Cellars" ("Podnimalis' iz t'my pogrebov," 1904), it is of slight interest when and where events take place: the focus is all but exclusively on the mood enveloping the dreariness and poverty of life in the big city. In one of Blok's most famous poems, "The Stranger," which is set in a suburb of Petersburg, the expression "every evening" appears three times, making time general rather than concrete and actual. The use of the plural makes locations unspecific: we read about "the restaurants," about the "boredom of suburban villas," about "level-crossings." Georg Heym in "The Demons of the City" discusses his nightmarish city in such terms as "a sea of houses," "streets," and "streetlamps." Eliot's "Rhapsody on a Windy Night" talks about "the street" and the "streetlamp," but the precise location is shrouded in obscurity. Here, too, phenomena typical of any city appear in the plural:

> Smells of chestnuts in the streets,
> And female smells in shuttered rooms,
> And cigarettes in corridors
> And cocktail smells in bars.

We have purely metaphorical imagery; every city object suggests an invisible force at work in the background (Barta 1986A).

In the modernist urban novel, the city also appears fragmented, but here a chorus of mutually interacting voices depicts it from many perspectives within the novel's dialogic discourse. While the city's image burdens the novel's consciousness as a metaphor, the metonymic interrelationship of specific details dominates the surface of the text. Bely's Petersburg, Joyce's Dublin and Döblin's Berlin stand out as condensed and specific figures of meaning.

The novels that will be discussed in greater detail in this book, *Petersburg*, *Ulysses*, and *Berlin Alexanderplatz*, form a subgenre within the tradition of the European modernist novel. The modernist techniques at work in the artistic construction of these novels foreground the figure of the city, allowing it to dominate narration, plot, and characters. The city outweighs in importance the roaming and confused characters, and the plot has no clear beginning and end. We shall discuss each novel in similar terms: questions will be raised regarding the pace of movement in the city; how the provocatively plural, "writable" text of the novel liberates the past enshrined in the space of the present; why walking is such a prominent activity in the characters' lives; and how desire provides the link between the human subject and the city.

The physical environment of the city, its history, and its political reality—ultimately responsible for its "atmosphere" and "personality"—determine the patterns of wandering. Gaston Bachelard argues in *The Poetics of Space* that human consciousness depends on the surrounding world of objects. He suggests that the contents of space into which one is born inform one's identity considerably (Bachelard 1964, 15). In the three novels, important motifs are connected with specific locations that play a special role in the lives of the walking characters: they attract or repel them and, for sure, preoccupy their thoughts. Some urban features become recurring motifs producing flashes of recognition that shed more light on events than the loose plot. When "epiphanic" moments uncover truths invisible in the weak temporal-causal development of the plot and the highly sketchy and impressionistic representation of three-dimensional urban reality, a transcendental dimension becomes active in the consciousness of these novels.

The concept of an invisible dimension—beyond the narrow positivist concept of "reality"—arises at the fin de siècle and in the early twentieth century, when art searches for new forms in which to convey spirituality. Dissatisfaction with positivism affects not only the arts but the sciences as well; increasing interest surrounds such problems as, for example, non-Euclidian geometry. Similarly to several of his Western contemporaries, the Russian Pyotr Demyanovich Uspensky suggests in his book, *Tertium Organum* (1911), that three-dimensionality is a product of the illusion provoked by our inability to measure the fourth dimension. Thus, the three-dimensional world shrouds the *noumenon*, the intangible "quintessence," in the phenomenon (Henderson 1983, 250–51).

Within this invisible dimension, the textual city incorporates space and time: the present, the past, and the implied future. Because of the presence of a mythic or a "fourth" dimension, the city's fragmentation is complete in the novel: the many experiences of the characters are complemented by the contents of their consciousness, which enter the text as independent agents. All this approximates to the chaotic sense of infinity (Long 1985, 154). The reader confronts multiple levels that, like the "cityscape," confuse; the dynamic cubist paintings create a similar effect. In the history of painting, cubism came closest to capturing depth on a surface. In Picasso's *Still Life* (1912), out of a medley of seemingly unrelated images, a more truthful representation of a violin arises than in any photo or realist painting (Gombrich 1950, 432–34). The images of the cities in the three texts have struck many readers as so expressive because the uneven modernist writing creates an impact analogous with many works by Kandinsky, Léger, Picasso, and Chagall.

The extensive use of metonymy in the written text produces collages: catalogues of things united solely by their adjacency. The walkers are important because they serve as points of reference amidst the haphazardly compiled, discordant, yet specific, city phenomena: they were seen by one or several people who happened to be in one particular place at a certain time. The walkers of these city novels, just like the flâneurs of the previous centuries, are all men. The prevalent male-dominated social order does not respect a woman's desire to roam about without purpose in the city. As in Gogol's "Nevsky Prospect" or "Overcoat," women walking the streets without a clear destination, particularly after dark, are prostitutes. Tolstoy's Anna Karenina, shortly before her suicide, drinks in with her eyes the spectacle of the hustle and bustle of Moscow but she does so only from behind the sheltering carriage windows. Once outside the carriage, as she wanders about the station, she becomes a spectacle for curious eyes to feast on. While Virginia Woolf's Mrs. Dalloway roams mainly within the confines of the mind, she is definitely one of the most famous literary walkers of London. But her movements are not purposeless and she is never outside her status of privilege, wealth, and physical safety. The female protagonist of Jean Rhys' *Good Morning, Midnight*, however, is a rootless and aimless pedestrian in the Paris streets. But here her similarity with the heroes of Bely's, Joyce's, and Döblin's novels ends. She cannot be an observer because she is so conspicuous as a woman attempting to be a flâneur: she is constantly watched, talked about, and pursued. Rather than turning her environment into a spectacle, she becomes an object of interest for those surrounding her. Thus, women in premodern and modernist prose are complements to men instead of subjects in their own right; they are denied the walker's prerogative to ramble and turn the city into an object of observation. Instead, other citizens turn the randomly wandering female into a commodity for men to use (Buck-Morss 1986, 119).

Bely's, Joyce's, and Döblin's walking characters combine features of both the respectable, educated flâneur and the badaud, whose sense of identity, background, and history are secondary in importance to his being at one with the crowds and the urban milieu. The modernist city novel's rambling heroes become readers of the haphazardly juxtaposed signs whose chain makes up the modern metropolis. These characters merge the themes of the eighteenth- and nineteenth-century flâneur and badaud with the age-old problem of homelessness. The walker is no longer an established man of leisure curiously pondering the contents of his visual impressions. The "purposeless" walk is, after all, endowed with purpose. Characters leave home because the traditional values of domesticity become meaningless to them. The protagonists who roam about the city's streets in these novels feel out of place and victimized. Walking about without a destination in mind becomes a purposeful activity as the walker looks upon the city as a replacement for the home. The walkers in the three novels leave their domestic space and move from the known towards the unknown. However familiar they may be with the topography, the city never ceases to be a mystery for them. It is as though these walkers were drawn towards an enigmatic center, lurking behind the multitude of entities making up the metropolis. Differently put, the characters are propelled to engage in sometimes frenzied, sometimes unhurried and aimless, movement about town because they feel deprived of some vital aspect of life. All the central characters are "seekers." Nikolai Apollonovich in Bely's *Petersburg* and Stephen Dedalus in Joyce's *Ulysses* cannot free themselves from their emotionally tormented childhood and adolescence; Joyce's Leopold Bloom is looking for a reunion with his past and the son he has lost; Bely's Senator Ableukhov is drawn to the sources of rebellion he attempts to control and repress in his capacity as a high-ranking official of the Establishment; Franz Biberkopf in Döblin's *Berlin Alexanderplatz* yearns hopelessly for the supposed joys and comforts of petit bourgeois life. They all try to live up to a long-cherished ideal of warmth and intimacy unavailable to them. Their sense of restlessness increases in their modern, twentieth-century setting; a nearly infinite number of possibilities of finding something hidden or lost lurk amidst the flotsam and jetsam of the city. The constant sense of missing your opportunity to find what you are searching for by being in the wrong place at the wrong time accounts for the intense nervousness that prevails. This experience is expressed with great sensitivity in the narrator's account of Stephen Dedalus' early wanderings about Dublin in *A Portrait of the Artist as a Young Man*: "A vague dissatisfaction grew up within him as he looked on the quays and on the river and on the lowering skies and yet he continued to wander up and down day after day as if he really sought someone that eluded him" (Joyce 1965, 66).

Thus, desire generates the wandering about the city. Behind purposeless rambling lies a wish to find wholeness. In Lacan's terms, the human subject is anguished by his lack; he looks for the other, the non-I, the "essence." The presumed hidden meaning lies in a signified towards which the signifying chain, comprised of the particles of the city, points. However, as poststructuralist theories argue, "meaning" or "signified" or the "center" escapes its own signification. The "center" in the novels discussed here is the unifying force that keeps the vast, messy entity of the city together and that accounts for all its mysteries.

Its marginal and disjointed sons and daughters depend on this "center" for their well-being, but it keeps forever hiding from them, in the gaps between its visible and concrete urban manifestations that surround people everywhere. The decentered modernist text, with its fragmented surface, circles—like the walkers—around this empty center that oppresses characters by fostering a desire that is never to be fulfilled.

CHAPTER 2

Knights and Unicorns
The Walkers of *Petersburg*

The most outstanding example of modernist prose in Russia's brief "Silver Age" is Andrei Bely's *Petersburg*. It never turned into a scholars' bestseller like James Joyce's *Ulysses*, nor did it enjoy widespread popularity with a broad reading public like Alfred Döblin's *Berlin Alexanderplatz*. The unusual syntax, vocabulary, and narrative manner of *Petersburg* never had the chance to generate a tradition of modernist novels in Russian, or to be discussed by schools of enthusiastic scholars and their pupils. The experimental artistic and literary movements in Russia failed to become broadly accepted as in the West; on the contrary, Russia's Communist rulers after October 1917 frowned upon modernism. They labeled such art as decadent and destructive, as an art removed from the real interests and needs of the people.

Bely's novel is no longer relegated to oblivion. During recent decades it has been published several times in Russian and in translation. In the 1970s and 1980s it gave rise to a substantial body of scholarship. Nevertheless, it has never been recognized as a prototype of the modernist city novel. Literary historians have reserved this place for *Ulysses*, admittedly the most influential of such novels. *Petersburg* had little or no impact on European literature in the 1920s and 1930s. Well before its first appearance in book form in 1916—six years before Joyce's *Ulysses*—Bely had published his *Four Symphonies* (1902). In 1959 Gleb Struve noted that "the *Second Symphony* was indeed *bahnbrechend*. It is a pity that this work is practically unknown outside Russia. If it were, it would be seen to anticipate some aspects of Joyce or such works as Virginia Woolf's *Mrs Dalloway* or *The Waves*" (1959, 465). Indeed, Bely's early work opened the way to the age of the twentieth-century experimental novel (Szilard 1967, 311).

Petersburg is the first modernist city novel, but it is also a monument of symbolist prose. One of the most apocalyptic novels in all Western literature, it draws on the literary myth of St. Petersburg which, most notably, Pushkin, Gogol, and Dostoevsky had sustained and enriched. According to the myth, Petersburg is a highly unusual city where human fate is determined by invisible, supernatural powers. Many of the unique features are attributed to the mysterious tsar, Peter the Great, who is responsible for the creation of the new capital. Bely's city symbolizes the fate of Russia, which is one of the novel's specific concerns. *Petersburg* overtly implies the presence of a transcendental intellect at work behind the image of the city. On a more general level, *Petersburg* embodies the idea that the twentieth-century city is the scene of the crisis of modern life. In his essay, "Circular Movement," Bely writes that "[o]ur life is Basel"; indeed, many details of his presentation of the Swiss city will strike readers of *Petersburg* as familiar (Maguire and Malmstad 1987, 106). The literary image of the bureaucratic, industrial, and commercial city's existence is made possible by its citizens; the contents of their isolated consciousness form the basis on which the modernist city novel builds. The artificial verbal recreation of Petersburg in the novel does not reflect, but rather explores, the actual city. The latter turns into text as its inhabitants' culture, memories, intuitions, hopes, and fears create the narrative and the characters. In all three city novels discussed in this book, the "external"/"objective" and the "internal"/"subjective" worlds become inseparably dependent on each other. The emphasis shifts from the plot—the narrated story, that is—to the process of narration: in other words, from *what* is being told to *how* it is being told.

The three novels offer compendia of incomplete images and unexplained metaphors. One critic, for instance, writes of *Petersburg* that no "cogent interpretation" has yet been provided (Anschuetz 1983B, 251); clearly, by the nature of the novel, no such satisfactory account can be undertaken. No univocal narratorial or authorial voice has absolute authority: the center of intelligence has all but disintegrated and the image of the city and the citizens contains a great variety of intentional and unintentional gaps and silences. Different readers' attempts to fill these gaps will, of course, vary considerably.

The story of *Petersburg*, like that of *Ulysses* or *Berlin Alexanderplatz*, is simple: a secret terrorist organization decides in October 1905 to take up Nikolai Apollonovich Ableukhov on his promise to assassinate his own father, Senator Apollon Apollonovich Ableukhov, a prominent state official. Nikolai Dudkin, a volunteer in the organization, is supposed to give a letter instructing the son to kill the father, together with a time bomb wrapped in a sardine tin. Dudkin delivers the bomb, but fails to hand over the letter, about whose contents he is ignorant. The letter then starts making its way to the Ableukhov son, and as its contents become known, it causes much confusion. Added to this is the unexpected arrival of Anna Petrovna Ableukhova, the mother who had previously left her family for an Italian lover. The bomb has been set; Dudkin in the meantime kills the author of the letter, Lippanchenko, who ordered this political murder. The bomb explodes but does not kill anyone. Dudkin goes insane, the Senator and his wife retire to the country to die, and Nikolai Apollonovich travels about in Egypt before returning to his country to roam the fields for the rest of his life, following the teachings of Skovoroda, the "Ukrainian Diogenes."

Other important characters include Sofia Petrovna Likhutina, the object of Nikolai Ableukhov's unrequited love, and her husband; Morkovin, the police double agent; and, last but not least, Falconet's statue, the Bronze Horseman who, according to Vyacheslav Ivanov, is the novel's leading character (1986, 209). All the action takes place in Petersburg; the characters move about town on foot or by carriage, and the text records the response of their consciousness to the urban environment. Like the Dostoevskian "dreamers" of the Petersburg street, Bely's citizens combine features of the Western European flâneur and his late successor, the badaud: they walk because no purpose-oriented, rational activity is available to them and they want to disappear and hide from a threatening force they cannot clearly define. Petersburg is in the foreground of their feverish consciousness. Unlike the city in *Ulysses* or in *Berlin Alexanderplatz*, Bely's Russian capital is primarily a nightmarish vision, and the movements of the characters seem to be taking place in a dream whose components have their foundations in the "Petersburg myth." Since the environment is inextricably bound up with the consciousness of Bely's characters, we will need to discuss how the setting of the perambulations radiates symbolical significance. The pattern and the motivation of the characters' movements can be viewed both as a condition and a result of the city's existence. Their trajectory follows a circle, originating in the home, going out into the city, and returning to the point of departure (in the Bronze Horseman's case, "home" is the base of the statue). The narrator coordinates the movement even as he accounts for it. He is more like a function than a character; his diverse voices cannot belong to one person. Since he is removed from the plot, and spends a large amount of time contemplating and observing in the streets of Petersburg, his often ironical perspective resembles that of the sensitive flâneur. The following passage reveals a narrating persona who sees himself as an outsider in the crowd he is observing:

> High above fly the cranes. City-dwellers cannot hear them in all the din; but they are flying over the city. Somewhere, on the Prospect, in speeding carriages and in the cries of newsboys, where automobiles raise throaty hoots—here, on the pavement, the inhabitant of the fields will stop as if rooted in the spot and incline his bearded head to one side:

"Shhh!"
"What is it?"
"Listen."
"What?"
"There . . . the cranes are calling."
. . . And a circle of gawking people forms, and the side-walk is blocked.
(220)[1]

Not only has he time to perceive more attentively than preoccupied walkers with business at hand, but he also has an eye for the unusual: the citizens rush about and grow estranged from nature, represented here by the cranes and by the peasant who is the only one interested in the birds.

We hear direct speech in dialogues and unmediated single voices that involve the reader maximally in making meaning. A similar role is played by the many extralinguistic narrative devices expressed in typographical experimentation. Throughout the text, instead of semantic units, ellipses and single question and exclamation marks surrounded by quotation marks make up entire lines (Tomei 1994). No Russian writer accomplished more in experimenting with the possibilities of typography than Bely (Janecek 1984, 29):

Playing on the crimson face was:
"?
"!
"!?" (253)

The narratorial function lacks a unique perspective. Instead of a "multivoiced" narrator, endowed with the ability to "shift from earthbound to visionary voices" (Alexandrov 1985, 54), we are dealing with a text that is "flooded with a host of different narrators who seem to create characters at will, now identifying with—now becoming distanced from them" (Keys 1983, 46). When the narrating persona parades as omniscient narrator, he comes across as the most versatile walker in the novel: he can follow several characters at the same time. For example, after the ball—where all the protagonists meet—he pursues several characters simultaneously: Nikolai Apollonovich and Morkovin—the police double agent—and then Sofia Petrovna and Apollon Apollonovich, even though the two go in different directions (the former towards the Summer Garden, the latter across the river to Vasilevsky Island). As he records events at, and after, the ball, and also inside the Likhutin flat, he captures Sofia Petrovna's return to her home both from inside and outside the building. His narration combines his own supposedly omniscient perspective with Sofia Petrovna's limited understanding of matters. Her grotesquely depicted yearning for well-being in a rational world contrasts with the narrating voice's awareness of a complex, partially invisible, multidimensional universe: "Indignantly the entry-way banged. Darkness enveloped her, the inexpressible enclosed her for an instant (this is how it probably is in the first second after one dies); but Sofia Petrovna Likhutina thought of death for not one second: on the contrary, she thought of ever so simple matters" (*Peterburg*, 175). The voice in this passage does not qualify as narratorial omniscience proper as in the highly developed psychological realism of Flaubert or Tolstoy; the narrator's hints and intimations assume less than full knowledge of the situation. Nor does the novel make use of the double viewpoint of "parallax" that characterizes *Ulysses*, in which Dublin on 16 June 1904 is viewed simultaneously by Stephen Dedalus and Leopold Bloom.

The implied author in *Petersburg* imposes cognitive restrictions on the narrator-function. Having been immersed in theosophy and then anthroposophy, Bely advocates the belief throughout the novel that consciousness creates form. He wishes to suggest the existence of a central, transcendental being whose mental activities create the Russian capital as well as the novel. The narrative voice in the novel refers to this process as "cerebral play." Things exist because they have been named, we learn from Bely's essay, "The Magic of Words." All "producers" of reality are themselves the product of somebody else's consciousness. Nothing is independent, according to Bely's theory, and this accounts for the bond between mythology and history, the past and the present, East and West, Bely and his implied author, the narrator-function and the characters, and most importantly, between the Russian capital and the city. The narrator creates characters by cerebral play and the characters, in turn, create each other in the same fashion. Apollon Apollonovich conjures up Dudkin beside his carriage, and the latter, visiting Nikolai Apollonovich, thinks of the Senator, who promptly appears at the gates of the house (Szilard 1984, 279). Cerebral play implies a "noumenon" in the invisible world from where the visible world originates. Cerebral play is analogous, moreover, with the function of the symbol in the text. In the view of the Russian symbolists we learn about "truth"—which is always transcendental—through symbols: they bring about and illuminate being through the activity of naming.

The text of *Petersburg*, however, is too dialogic to tolerate the control the author imposes through his own understanding of the world; the novel shows all the features of what Bakhtin calls multivoicedness, and this effectively dilutes any "transcendental truth" (Keys 1983, 46). Maguire and Malmstad warn critics of Bely not to try to impose a narrow interpretation on his text: "If we attempt to find a philosopher's stone in Bely (or worse, outside him altogether, say in anthroposophy), we fail: readings of Bely must honor his addiction to plurality" (1987, 144). The narrative voices, and the characters, produce images of reality that do not recognize any hierarchy of ontological values as they cohabit the novel's consciousness. In the prologue, we hear at least two aspects of the storytelling voice. (Johannes Holthusen is right in suggesting that the prologue is a stylistic parody of Gogol's "skaz" narration; 1979, 286.) Both syntactically and lexically, the last paragraph differs markedly from the jesting manner of the previous ones. The reader is told about the "real plane"—the physical aspects—and the "fantastic plane"—the metaphysical aspects—of Petersburg (Steinberg 1978, 528). While the storyteller uses parody in presenting the "real plane," he adopts an awe-inspiring manner when dealing with the invisible, astral, metaphysical, fourth-dimensional realm. Bely, of course, draws on his knowledge of fashionable occult theories; Carlson has suggested that some theosophists considered the astral plane the same as the "fourth dimension" (1993, 200-01). Throughout the novel, the narration ranges from "skaz" (narration that draws attention to the narrator's voice and the artificiality of narration in the text) to lofty rhetoric. In the latter mode, the narrator avoids parody and interjects pathos to relate "serious" matters: "As for Petersburg it will sink. In those days all the peoples of the earth will rush forth from their dwelling places. Great will be the strife, strife the like of which has never been seen in this world. The yellow hordes of Asians will set forth from their age-old abodes and will encrimson the fields of Europe in oceans of blood. There will be, oh yes, there will—Tsushima! There will be—a new Kalka! Kulikovo Field, I await you!" (65). Roger Keys argues that expressions such as the one quoted above are no more than personal beliefs, even if spoken by the narrating voice rather than a character, and that they simply add one more voice to the heteroglossia of the novel (Keys 1990, 5). As the voices of the narrator and the many characters offer different perspectives, they neutralize the word of authority in the text (Keys 1983, 46). The chatty narrator in the subsection "Our Role," the narrator exclaiming "Kulikovo Field, I await you!" and the storytelling voices mediating characters' otherworldly experiences all merge within the polyphonic text. We will find no "final" answers in *Petersburg* as in all texts: what the poststructuralists call the "transcendental signified" slips away and cannot be stated. The polyphony of the novel overrides all individual voices, however authoritative.[2] The novel's characters wander about in the city, but they undergo a common Petersburg experience rather than many individual experiences. The plural discourse of the novel seems, in fact, to chime in with the voice of the city.

In Bely's Petersburg, passers-by hear an ominous and threatening "ooo" sound of unknown origin, symbolizing destruction and chaos. Mysterious appearances originate in the same imagined center from which the source of cerebral play surges. This central point gives rise to Bely's symbolism: "Petersburg not only appears to us, but actually does appear—on maps: in the form of two small circles, one set inside the other, with a black dot in the center; and from precisely this mathematical point, which has no dimension, it proclaims forcefully that it exists: from here, from this very point surges and swarms the printed book; from this invisible point speeds the official circular" (2). This invisible point—outside the world of physical senses—accounts both for the Russian state, ruled and regulated from the capital, and also for all the city's irrational features. We know from Bely's essay, "The Emblematics of Meaning," that he believed everything that exists forms a part of an unknowable essence. In the essay "Ivanov," Bely explains the nature of his "fantastic method": as a result of the interaction of particles of everyday events, a more complex reality arises in fantastic images (1911, 405). Clearly, Bely echoes Vyacheslav Ivanov's motto, *a realibus ad realiora* (from things real to a higher reality). The novel's mysterious elements constantly hint at the existence of, but also disguise, a "more complex reality." The various appearances of Peter the Great around Petersburg (the Bronze Horseman riding down the street; the tall Dutchman; the boatman aboard his schooner, the Bronze Guest, visiting Dudkin at night), the "White Domino," and the "Persian" visitor Shishnarfne arise as creations of the minds ("cerebral play") of the "real" characters as they walk about their mysterious city or retire into their rooms to rest their overstrained brains. According to the occult principles underpinning theosophy and anthroposophy, when thoughts emanating from the consciousness of people in the physical world assume an existence of their own in the "astral" sphere, these thoughts will have direct impact on the "real" events of the physical world (Carlson 1993, 202).

The feverish pace of wandering and the frenzied cerebral activity, however, do not accomplish the desired results. A critic speaks of a species, the *"homo peterburgiensis"*: people hurrying about in the service of contradicting causes, but all belonging to the same city, however great their sense of animosity towards each other (Klotz 1969, 284). Some busy themselves arranging a revolution, while others rush about to prevent them from doing so. Government circulars emerge from a dot in Senator Ableukhov's brain; his adversaries concentrate destructive power into a dot in a sardine tin to destroy him and his regime. Both efforts fail. The circulars do nothing to prevent the revolutionary movement from descending upon the center from the islands and the country's vast expanses. In the meantime, the anarchists cannot even control their own bomb, unable to manage either its timing or its destructive power. In spite of the constant movement about town, going from one place to another does not help people solve their problems: Bely's characters serve as extensions of the contradictions that pervade the city and Russian society, and whose roots—channels of cerebral play, Bely would have us think—lead to transcendental intelligence.

Events in *Petersburg* take place during October 1905. Clearly, Bely's work offers no mimetic representation of historical events. In "The Inspiration of Horror," an article on *Petersburg*, Vyacheslav Ivanov praises the novel's "spiritual energy," and "prophetic significance" (1986, 209). It would seem that this "fundamental force" causes all the tension, miscommunication, and the revolution itself rather than being a result thereof. Let us survey the conflicts that propel the feverish pace of movement. Senator Ableukhov feels socially embarrassed and personally unhappy because of his broken marriage. The revolutionary activity he senses even in his own son's highly suspicious behavior terrifies him. Meanwhile, the near-hysterical son, in his sexual frustration, pursues Sofia Petrovna.[3] Assuming that Sofia Petrovna summoned him to a secret assignation in the Summer Garden, he finds Varvara Evgrafovna waiting for him. She, in turn, pursues Nikolai, but her love for him remains unrequited. Dudkin, an activist, inadvertently in the service of double agents, tries to catch up with Nikolai Apollonovich. He wants to persuade him to throw into the river the bomb he had given him earlier not knowing that it was designed to enable the young Ableukhov to kill his father. Later, Nikolai Apollonovich mistakenly assumes that Sofia's husband, Lieutenant Likhutin, is chasing him across town out of jealousy, and, thus, fails to return home to defuse the now activated time bomb. Amidst the chaos that Anna Petrovna Ableukhova's return has caused, the Senator loses the ticking time bomb that he obtained earlier while going through his son's personal belongings.

The ever-present symbolism suggests the transcendental origin of all the confusion, chaos, and nervousness. However, Bely limits his perspective to a highly selective set of attributes of Petersburg: the whole city is not accessible to him (Berdyaev 1986, 198). Because of the nature of the metropolis, no one person can know the near-infinite aspects that comprise it and produce the "spirit" of the place. While sensitive and attentive observers, no doubt, perceive and detect the spiritual center, no one can locate it. As a result of this particular city's brief and unconventional history, and the myth about its foundation and destiny, attempts to attribute confusion and unhappiness to transcendental, even cosmic, disharmony have culturally greater appeal than in

Joyce's Dublin or Döblin's Berlin. Bely draws on this to great effect as he conceives the city for his novel.

Bely's Petersburg, then, was envisaged as a "mask" over the abyss. Nietzsche's *Birth of Tragedy* had a strong impact on the Russian symbolists and Bely's own thinking reflects Nietzsche's influence. We know from *The Memoirs of an Eccentric* that, according to Bely, "[t]he sole significance of the architectonics, of the phrase, is to avert the reader's eye from the sacred point: the genesis of myth" (quoted from Alexandrov 1985, 99). Thus, in Bely's view, we see a veil in this world, protecting us from what we are not supposed to know. The novel's parodistic level suggests that the Russian state also "protects" the citizens through its regulations. One of its senior bureaucrats, this novel's central character, is called "Apollon," clearly alluding to Nietzsche's concept of the "Apollonian" (Barta 1991–92). On the novel's parodistic level, red and white dominoes appear in the streets of the city. Their opposition as representatives of the division between order, harmony, and Christ, on the one hand (White Domino), and chaos, "Mongolism," and the Antichrist, on the other (Red Domino), is ironical. Ineffective figures both, they represent no metaphysical or eschatological force. Nevertheless, the White Domino appears shrouded in obscurity. He is "tall" and "sad," with vaguely Christlike attributes. Yet, he solves nothing and helps no one; at critical moments he disappears or turns out to be someone else. Dudkin hears a neighbor address the figure as "Misha." The White Domino meets Nikolai Apollonovich on Nevsky Prospect and makes a powerful impression on him: "And it seemed as if someone sad, whom Nikolai Apollonovich had never seen before, had entered his soul, and that the bright light of his eyes had begun to pierce him. Nikolai Apollonovich shuddered. 'You all pursue and persecute me!' 'What?' He tried to catch the voice: 'I look after all of you. . . .' . . . There was no possessor of the voice" (220). In fact, the "voice" leads to, or rather its owner turns out to be, Likhutin. The name "Misha" in connection with Likhutin as the White Domino is not accidental: the motif of the duel of Archangel Michael with the Devil is present in the parodistic struggle between Nikolai Ableukhov and Lieutenant Likhutin. Of course, owing to the novel's complex symbolist scheme, Nikolai Apollonovich can also appear as Christlike: in the course of their battle, Likhutin's face expresses a "devilish smile," suggesting that his opponent is Christ (Szilard 1984, 606). It has also been argued that in the figure of the White Domino Bely makes a self-conscious reference to himself; after all, the pseudonym "Andrei Bely" means Andrew the White. In his capacity as author, he clearly "looks after all his characters, deny him though they may." After the ball, the White Domino turns out to be a policeman (Garvey 1985, 185–86). As a further possible analogy between the writer and the police, it is noteworthy that in the subchapter "Our Role" the narrating persona suggests that he will undertake the role of the Secret Police as he follows the "stranger" (22). In general, the White Domino is a figure of confusion; his intervention as Nikolai Apollonovich is supposed to rush home to defuse the bomb demonstrates this well. The White Domino's assistance to Sofia Petrovna also adds to, rather than resolves, the tension. The carriage he catches to take her home rushes down the embankment. Sofia Petrovna has a terrifying experience as she does not know where she is being taken and the Bronze Horseman is chasing her carriage: "There was the pounding of a metallic steed, with a ringing clatter against stone. Behind her he was trampling everything that had flown off. There, behind her back, the metallic Horseman had started up in pursuit" (120). Confusion also results from the Red Domino's activities. His donning the mask and the costume fails to advance his attempt to seduce Sofia Petrovna. He causes confusion at the ball, though, particularly for his father. Furthermore, he makes it into the gossip columns of the newspapers, but accomplishes nothing else.

According to authorial logic, citizens in *Petersburg* cannot but falter between contradictory forces. Like the Red and the White Dominos, opposing ideologies, arising from the same center of intelligence, keep reinforcing each other and destroying the people in their respective camps. According to Bely's theory of color symbolism, the color white is a hidden red. He writes in "Sacred Colors": "It is well known in physics that white light can turn red when it crosses an ashy, nontransparent substance of a certain thickness and consistency. The relationship of white light to grey substance brings about this impression of red" (1910, 119–20, my translation). No wonder that characters experience a sense of *mise en abîme*. Senator Ableukhov certainly does when going to sleep; his son feels on the edge of another "space-time" when dozing off on the sardine tin with the "horrible content," that is, the time bomb. Lippanchenko, the police double agent, senses the abyss minutes before his death, and his victim and murderer in one person, Dudkin, does so just before the "Bronze Horseman" pays him a visit.

The statue as a walker of the Petersburg streets, interacting with "Evgeny" Dudkin, among others, establishes an effective intertextual dialogue with Pushkin's "Bronze Horseman." Indeed, the statue embodies the plural nature of Bely's city most clearly. The frightening, "Dionysian" activities of the anthropomorphic Bronze Horseman madden the city-dweller. Not only is the statue brought to life but it also embodies an ominous force that crushes individual freedom:

The face of the Horseman and the bronze laurel wreath flared. And a many-tonned arm extended imperiously. It seemed that the arm was about to move, and that metallic hooves at any moment would come crashing down upon the crag, and through all of Petersburg would resound:

"Yes, yes, yes . . .

It is—I . . .

"I doom: irrevocably!"

For a moment everything was suddenly flooded with light for Nikolai Apollonovich. Yes, he understood: he must. Roaring with laughter he fled from the Bronze Horseman. (149)

In its emphatic allusion to Pushkin's Peter, however, Bely's statue also has a different side to its "personality" since it can sometimes act on behalf of harmony and "order": the "Bronze Guest" puts Dudkin at ease even as it commissions him to murder Lippanchenko, who has ordered the parricide, the most tangible cause of conflict in the novel.

Peter's figure, then, radiates contradiction; his mysterious boat emits a symbolical "rosy-colored steam." Rose or "pinkish" (137) vapors are the result of mixing red and white. The merger of different qualities is also conveyed in the symbolism of names. Apollon Apollonovich protects "Apollonian" order in the state apparatus that Peter the Great established. His surname, Ableukhov, points to the family's Mongol (Tartar) origin and, therefore, embodies the principle of destruction, at least according to a popular racist theory regarding Asia that prevailed among Russian symbolists. Nikolai Apollonovich vowed to help the "revolutionaries," to bring down the Western power hierarchy that Peter the Great had introduced, but as a student of Kant, he is thoroughly immersed in the Western order he is seeking to destroy (Cioran 1973, 142–51). Dudkin's name derives from the word "dudka," which means "pipe." In spite of this strongly "Dionysian" attribute in his surname, he not only reads the biblical book of the Apocalypse but also acts as the mythological Tsar Peter's agent in killing Lippanchenko, who issued Senator Ableukhov's death sentence: "Greetings, my son!" the Bronze Horseman says to Dudkin (214).

The same division that torments people is also apparent in the city's environment and architecture. People perceive space around them as fathomless; vapors, mists, and blinding glitter prevent them from seeing clearly. Communication is unsuccessful; walls do not seal properly. The spacious and grand neoclassical central part of Petersburg, where the ministries and the residences of the Tsar and the wealthiest people are, expresses a sharp contrast with the dark, foggy "islands" across the river where the workers and low-ranking bureaucrats—in short, poor people—live. However, throughout the novel, characters constantly wander from one to the other; confusion infiltrates both parts with equal force.

Humans most usually walk in order to get from one place to another on foot. In *Petersburg*, as in *Ulysses* and *Berlin Alexanderplatz*, the motivation to wander about the city frequently lies in the wish to avoid the home. Gaston Bachelard in *The Poetics of Space* doubts that city dwellings are able to offer the phenomenological values of the house in the country (1964, 42), but he makes no real effort to evaluate residences in large urban areas. *Petersburg*, together with *Ulysses* and *Berlin Alexanderplatz*, provides a thorough "phenomenology" of domestic space in the metropolis. While the primary task here is not to analyze this feature of the modernist city novel, it will be necessary to investigate the nature of dwelling places in the fictional portraits of these cities; after all, the protagonists feel unsafe, uncomfortable and unhappy at home, which is why they prefer to walk.

In fact, the "out-of-doors" in Bely's *Petersburg* exhibits the same repressive qualities as the home. Nikolai Apollonovich rushes to the Summer Garden from his domestic unhappiness. There, however, he finds deception bred by miscommunication. The scenery that surrounds him is described as follows: "The Summer Garden lay somber. The statues each stood hidden beneath boards. The boards looked like coffins standing on end. The coffins lined the paths. Both nymphs and satyrs had taken shelter in them, so that the tooth of time might not gnaw them away with frost. Time sharpens its teeth for everything—it devours body and soul and stone" (97). The classical statues give the garden its character. They spend the best part of the autumn and the spring and all the winter months in coffin-like brown, wooden boxes that protect them from the reality of nature—wet, foggy, windy weather, constant cold moisture in the air—in short, from the conditions that make the area unfit for human habitation. These gracious neoclassical figures, attempting to depict the Mediterranean ancestors of Western culture, live in dark containers in the Neva's northern marshlands. They symbolize the concept of the "home" in *Petersburg*, surrounded by walls that do not shelter, like the wooden boxes with their cracks and holes. The narrator emphasizes Peter the Great's responsibility for the fate of the city: "Peter himself had planted this garden, watering the balsamine and mint with his own hand" (97).

Peter's "Apollonian" descendant, Senator Ableukhov, is perhaps the most enclosure-bound character of the novel. For the most part, he is no walker; he likes closed, securely surrounded sites, such as the toilet (the place "comparable to no other") and his black carriage. Only clearly defined and artificial geometrical units—cubes and parallelograms—make him feel at ease. He can work, that is, order and rule, only in his secure boxes, in the office and in the carriage. The name "Apollon Apollonovich" as an allusion to the Greek Apollo creates a somewhat parodistic effect: the Senator's physical looks befit the classical god of artistic beauty no more than the wooden boxes match the appearance of the statues in the Summer Garden. However, Apollo was also the god of mice, and the old and withered Senator not only has a fondness for mice but also cuts a grayish figure, like a mouse, in his domestic environment. The Senator has, however, some significant, nonparodistic, attributes which relate him, and the official Petrine Establishment he serves, to Apollo. Some of the less familiar features of the Greek god connect him with urban civilization in an inhospitable natural environment. In Aeschylus's *Eumenides*, Apollo is referred to as a "road builder"; Apollo "Agyieus," furthermore, is the patron of streets and vouches for their safety. From Aristophanes' *Wasps* we know that a statue of Apollo would be put up in the doorway, marking the boundary between inside and outside as a form of protection (Barta 1991–92, 396; Steinberg 1977, 143). However, the Senator is unsuccessful in achieving his Apollonian desire to have safety and protection surrounding his "civilized values" in the intimacy of his home; both mentally and physically he is at greatest risk in his own house.

Apollon Apollonovich attempts to apply his theories to protecting his state and his home. In his house, he has arranged his personal belongings in boxes and drawers, following a systematic order. His ideal plan for a city is purely geometric; it is easy to control any form of unrest on the part of the citizens in a town of straight lines and blocks. Senator Ableukhov's thinking here matches that of the architects of Petersburg and also that of Baron Haussmann, who remodeled Paris. However, wide, open places, including the large and spacious rooms in his own house, fill Apollon Apollonovich with terror. His tall windows look out on the river and the threatening islands. He dislikes his house and would rather live somewhere smaller and narrower where it is easier to hide.

A strong correspondence prevails between the furniture and interior design of homes and the internal turmoil of their occupants. Senator Ableukhov decorated his house with small statues, shining surfaces, and armor: "From all sides golden pier glasses swallowed the drawing room in greenish mirror surfaces. They were crowned by the wings of cute little golden-cheeked cupids. A small mother-of-pearl table glittered.... [Apollon Apollonovich's] step tapped along the gleaming panels of parquetry.... The parquetry gleamed" (6–8). The decoration reflects the wish to re-create a European atmosphere; the Senator's quarters have a decidedly Western look. The opposite taste dominates in his son's rooms and in Sofia Likhutina's flat. The wild colors, the Asian objects, the Japanese features all signify a challenge to the Petrine Establishment, symbolizing revolution and violence: "Tartar slippers were introduced.... Nikolai Apollonovich was wearing a Tartar skullcap (27–28).... [w]hen ... Sofia Petrovna Likhutina, wearing a pink kimono, flew from behind the door to the alcove, she was the perfect image of a real Japanese girl.... From the walls tumbled cascades, of the brightest, most irrepressible colors ... on the walls were Japanese fans" (39). Both the attempted classical harmony of the senatorial residence and the overheated, intentionally confusing, "oriental" home of Likhutina express a sharp contrast with the impoverished, insect-ridden, and sparsely furnished tiny room that Evgeny Dudkin rents in the other part of town, on Vasilevsky Island.

But Dudkin and Apollon Apollonovich are not the only ones who dislike their lodgings. In spite of the close resemblance between the professed ideologies of the inhabitants and the objects in their rooms, the novel's protagonists feel unsafe indoors and try to get away (Klotz 1969, 280). A stifling atmosphere transcending social and cultural differences prevails in every home. Lonely Dudkin in his Dostoevskian squalor, as well as members of the Ableukhov family in their opulent, aristocratic setting live isolated lives, and their inadequate communication imprisons them in the solitude of the self. People sleep alone and unloved. Lieutenant Likhutin feels like an unwelcome visitor in his wife's rooms; Apollon Apollonovich cannot breathe in Nikolai's room, who, in turn, finds his father's quarters terrifying. Senator Ableukhov flees from home to avoid his son's cold, reptilian, and unloving stare; furthermore, he also prefers not to have to see furniture, the piano and other objects, reminding him of his wife and their broken marriage.

The descriptions of Dudkin's room combine the naturalist's emphasis on the repulsive with the psychoanalyst's interest in the world of nightmares. Dudkin associates the yellow color of the wallpaper in his room with insomnia. Furthermore, "insomnia evoked the memory of a fateful face with very narrow little Mongol eyes. The face had looked repeatedly at him from the wallpaper. When he examined this place during the day, he could make out only a damp spot, over which crawled a sow bug" (26). His fear at home prompts him to rush out into the open. The streets of the police-controlled imperial capital do not offer protection from the law of which Dudkin is afraid as a revolutionary. But he is more frightened still by the heavy oppressiveness of his rented room. Outdoors and indoors form a vicious circle for Dudkin, though. The now "omniscient" voice of the narrator explains: "Alexander Ivanovich's observations had led him to the thought that peace at night depends on how you spend the day. You bring home with you what you have experienced on the streets, in squalid restaurants, in tearooms" (63–64). It is not surprising that he is distressed by his observations as a walker in the city, as he has dreadful dreams and visions at home. The novel's "occult" experiences tend to take place in the enclosed room where people perceive the sensation of being "locked in" most intensely. Dudkin, Nikolai Apollonovich, and the Senator are aware of "cerebral play": their thoughts become alive on the "astral plane" and this expanding process does not recognize such barriers as walls, doors, or windows. The Ableukhovs, in their attempt to accommodate the Western principle of individualism, feel like "centers of the universe" when they are surrounded by controllable, small space. However, they have no control over "expansion." In his parodistic mood, the narrator informs us that besides cerebral play, the Senator's inner organs spread out as well: his expanded heart and expanding gases undermine his desire to "[soar] above the Universe like Zeus" from his office. The Ableukhovs and Dudkin find no rest when they fall asleep; the expanding energy that propels restlessness all day does not cease at night. Even when asleep, the activity of walking does not stop; now it occupies the vertical rather than the horizontal dimension. In bed, at night, Apollon Apollonovich's dreaming consciousness enters its "second space." We learn from the narrating voice that he goes on an "astral" journey through a corridor extending from his head, reflecting theosophist claims that consciousness brings about form and thought creates matter (Carlson 1993, 200). Nikolai Apollonovich also enters this astral realm (Piskunov 1987, 147). The "fourth-dimensional" energy in the city does not allow human subjects to enjoy unshared, private space even at night. As the old Senator lies in his bed, ready to sleep and devoid of the masks he needs both in his public and domestic lives, the expanding "world soul" leaps out of his body, urging him to go on an "astral walk." He flies out of his sad and lonely room to another dimension where gloom is "pretemporal":

> [H]e would pull up the blanket in order to embark upon a journey, for sleep is a journey. . . .
> Apollon Apollonovich always saw *two* spaces: one, material (the walls of the room, of the carriage), the other, not exactly spiritual (it was also material). Now, how should I put it: over Ableukhov's head, Ableukhov's eyes saw

bright patches and dots of light, and iridescent dancing spots with spinning centers. They obscured the boundaries of the spaces. Thus one space swarmed in the other space; you know, the kind that seems to be made of Christmas tree tinsel, of little stars and of little sparks. (93; italics in the original)

In their astral realm, when asleep, both father and son meet the "Turanian," their "ancestor," who appears in the shape of Apollon Apollonovich to Nikolai and as Nikolai Apollonovich to the Senator. As the walls in Bely's city do not seal, the out-of-doors of Petersburg also appears as inner space, just of a different kind. In mythic consciousness, Peter the Great's idea of the city resembles the image of the house in the wilderness. It is supposed to shelter Peter's re-creation of Western civilization in an incongruous and hostile environment. Yet, in contrast to city novels of the eighteenth and nineteenth centuries, where all inhabitants rushed home in the face of danger, in *Petersburg* they run away from their quarters when they feel ill at ease (Klotz 1969, 283). This is also the case in Joyce's *Ulysses* and Döblin's *Berlin Alexanderplatz*.

Of course, much of the time people walk about on their own. From the viewpoint of the organizing consciousness of the novel, it is clear that one person's activity annihilates the results of another's labor. Dudkin pursues Nikolai Apollonovich to give him the bomb and, later, to get him to defuse it; the Bronze Horseman gallops to the terrified Dudkin to readopt him, and also to commission him to kill the one who ordered the parricide. The double agents are out in the street earning salaries from both their employers, the police, and the secret society. But more interesting for the focus of this study are the numerous occasions when characters engage in seemingly aimless sauntering. Apollon Apollonovich, for one, frowns upon such "irrationality." And yet, the shocking events of the evening at the ball prompt even him to engage in "purposeless" walking.

This incident merits special attention: the Senator resents the open space so much that he tends never to go for a walk. After his own son turns out to be the Red Domino and Apollon Apollonovich's chances for promotion diminish, he also finds out from the obviously well-informed secret policeman—a double agent—that assassination plans are under way against him. Amidst all this, he has sent his carriage away and decides not to go home but to wander about. He sets off for Vasilevsky Island. Clearly, even during the day he has no business there, let alone at night; he finds the place disconcerting. The houses in the "islands" seem to him to be scattered in contrast to the ordered, straight geometrical streets in the center of Petersburg that he knows so well from his carriage window. Now, "[b]efore him was the outline of a miserable little rotting fence. . . . [A]ll spaces had been displaced, and the life of the 'solid citizen' was around him on all sides as gateways" (138). The Senator's conscious self embodies the *principium individuationis* of Nietzsche's Apollo in *The Birth of Tragedy*. But, at this moment of crisis, his subconscious self is in control, forcing him to disappear into the dark, Dionysian mess of the St. Petersburg night. Here, like Dudkin, he is just one amid millions instead of standing out as the distinguished and hated statesman, the one chosen to be assassinated. His assassin, Nikolai Apollonovich, makes as ostentatious a walker as his father: the gait of each is so individualistic that this feature alone makes them recognizable from a distance.

Walking, however, enables Dudkin, the flawless Petersburg walker ("pedestrianus petersburgiensis") to disappear. As the two "sons" of Apollo, opposed to the Ableukhovs, Dudkin, Dionysus' "descendant," feels at home in the messy crowd, and he easily manages to melt into the flow of the street and stay unnoticed: "[Dudkin] had an urge to get out of the room—into the dingy fog, there to merge with the shoulders, backs, greenish faces on a Petersburg prospect. . . . He had to pace from prospect to prospect, from street to street, until the brain was numbed" (170). The sight of the heap of shoulders and backs in the street pleases and soothes Dudkin. The same sight strikes Apollon Apollonovich as unbearable when a demonstrating mob blocks his way and he is forced to alight from his carriage on Nevsky Prospect. This crowd seems to exist by its own instinctive laws without any need of distinctive individuals: "Individual thought was sucked into the cerebration of the myriapod being that moved along the Nevsky. And wordlessly they stared at the myriad legs; and the sediment crawled. It crawled by and shuffled on flowing feet; the sticky sediment was composed of individual segments; and each individual segment was a torso. There were no people on the Nevsky, but there was a crawling, howling myriapod there" (179). It is a recurring motif in *Petersburg* that walkers and their accoutrements lose their distinct outline in the fog. Gogol's Petersburg enriches the intertextual consciousness of the novel; instead of figures, Bely writes about shadows and metonymically assembled parts. Legs, limbs, backs, noses, hats, and ears walk down the streets and across the bridges.

Berdyaev refers to an "antipersonalist" bias in Bely (1962, 233). Indeed, the characters in the novel do appear as incomplete personalities, resembling human shadows, or in other words, they undergo a process of "dynamic fragmentation" (Flaker 1976, 478). They form part of a vast intertextual network of Russian literature and classical mythology. All characters are shadows of somebody else's thoughts; this is consistent with Bely's theory of cerebral play. The *Redende Namen* also help to turn them into two-dimensional forms. The two

Ableukhovs merely shadow rather than embody aspects of Apollo: their Apollonian features are inconsistent with their actions. People in the street comment about Nikolai Apollonovich's resemblance to the Belvedere Apollo. When he is dressed up as the Red Domino, however, his behavior is violent and destructive. Yet his representation of Dionysus is lackluster and two-dimensional. Ironically, Bely entitled a subdivision in chapter 6 "Dionysus"; Nikolai Apollonovich appears here as particularly pitiful. Instead of having complete human personalities, Bely's people are like puppets, imperfectly and often parodistically copying aspects of ideological systems (Drozda 1981, 143 and 146). Even the narrator is a function rather than a person with a voice. The storytelling voice features several shadows: aspects of the Gogolian "skaz" narrator, and qualities of the implied author or an omniscient narrator, to name just the most obvious ones.

While the people seem to be less than human, grotesquely, Petersburg is very much alive. Surrealistic imagery activates the city and transforms people into passive matter. Nevsky Prospect turns into a "caviar sandwich." Similarly to the figure of the myriapod, the metaphor of the "caviar sandwich" also suggests the annihilation of the individual. References to caviar, and fish in general, are associated with the concept of explosion; the time bomb keeps ticking away in a sardine tin. Fish is "ryba" in Russian, and in the novel's vocal symbolism, "y" symbolizes vulgarity and sliminess.[4]

References are made to parts of the body, suggesting that human entities are incomplete or that they fall apart, as in an explosion. A sense of dealing with fragments instead of individuals prevents successful communication still further: "He began to shout at the back: 'Mm . . . listen here!' The back paid no heed. 'But stop!' It turned its head, and, recognizing the senator, ran to meet him (it was not the back running to meet him, but rather, the back's possessor . . .)" (129). The loss of clear outlines, in fact, typifies most literary works about St. Petersburg: the city's climate produces frequent fogs, vapor, and mists. Bely makes the most of the environment to produce his symbolic cityscape. The dark-green, sometimes black, waters of the bacilli-infested rivers and canals inform the novel's fundamental imagery. Winds howl over the waters and the cold rain seems to penetrate the very bones of walkers. They seldom see proper daylight. The night's darkness, with the city's artificial illumination, and hazy twilight in the mornings and evenings create the dominant impression. The foggy rains dim the streetlamps outside the city center, while the faint lights both inside and outside the houses help to create a mood of gloom and despondency. All colors, except for white, tend towards black, which, to Bely, indicates discord and doom in the world (Steinberg 1979).

Red is "blood-red" in *Petersburg*. The undeniable beauty of the actual city is all but completely neglected in the novel: descriptions suggest violence first and foremost. Because of their central location, the gold-colored tapering spires of the Admiralty and the Peter-Paul Fortress—constant reminders of Peter the Great—attract the attention of the characters as they walk about; these sights are visible from almost all points of the city. The domes, spires, and roofs glitter and shine in the daylight, which, according to the ironical comment of the narrating voice, is whiter than electricity. Most of the time, however, when the sun is not out, roofs and domes appear deathly green, shrouded in fog.

In spite of the numerous references to well-known places in St. Petersburg, the city in the novel is indeed different from the Russian capital in 1905. The fictional Petersburg, too, is a shadow. A critic talks about "realistic unreality" when describing this phenomenon (Dolgopolov 1977, 253): while the novel retains topographical accuracy in its overall depiction of the capital, the combination of details differs from what a visitor finds when going to the city. Although Bely was a Muscovite and did not live in Petersburg when writing the novel, he clearly knew the capital very well. The "inaccuracies," where the literary image deviates from the city on the map, amount to an intentional demonstration of the cerebral play that occurs in Peter's city.

To Russia's symbolists, the capital's mythical status strongly outweighed Petersburg's social and political realities. Vyacheslav Ivanov wrote in his essay, "The Inspiration of Horror": "Petersburg has only a conditional existence: it is an entity of reason and at the same time it is the meeting point of the forces which produce the variegated and universal Russian delusion" (1986, 208). Through remarkably subtle descriptions of exterior and interior details, we come to see the city as subjective space. The text draws upon actual urban architecture and climate. For all the novel's literary and mythological associations, it describes phenomena characteristic of the city in 1905. Clearly, a revolution is getting under way; strikes are taking place, and official cars sweep with feverish haste along electrically illuminated streets (Steinberg 1978, 524–25). Thanks to the many references to familiar sights, the city is recognizable in the novel; however, well-known places appear in a most peculiar combination, creating a sense that the existence of Bely's Russian capital is indeed conditional. When Sofia Petrovna and Varvara Evgrafovna are going to a political meeting, they walk down the Moika, past the Summer Garden. On their way, they see the Troitsky Bridge, the Winter Palace, and the dome of the Isaac Cathedral. The narrative combines these topographical details in such an implausible way that the walkers' location and direction cannot be determined at any time. Furthermore, we have no way of knowing where Senator Ableukhov's office is. The text positions the Ableukhov family residence in three different places. Firstly, the narrator refers to the house on the Gagarin Embankment, and then, in the seventh chapter, it is to be found on the English Embankment. When Nikolai and his father reach the gate of their house at the same time following their wanderings at night, they enter through a porch. Neither on the Gagarin nor on the English Embankment is there a house to be found with a porch. In the first and fifth chapters, Dudkin lives on the 17th Line on Vasilevsky Island; in the fourth chapter, however, we are told that his address is on the 18th Line (Dolgopolov 1977, 260–69).

Furthermore, Bely places certain objects, typical of the city and endowed with special signifying powers, incongruously in his *Petersburg*. Characters walk past Atlases and caryatids. These Greek mythological figures, used as supporting columns in neoclassical architecture, remind onlookers of the westernizing intention of the city's founder. The tension between outward form and substance founds the symbolist interpretation of both the Petersburg myth and these columns. The caryatids were dancers who performed in honor of the goddess Artemis, Apollo's twin sister. In Nietzsche's *Birth of Tragedy*, Apollo and Dionysus are presented as contradictory forces. To Bely an activity such as dance—presumed to be associated with Dionysus and here performed for Apollo's sister—probably suggests the inner contradiction within the phenomenon. (Nietzsche's and the Russian Symbolists' assumption about the opposition of the two gods may be philologically inaccurate; in many Greek myths, which *The Birth of Tragedy* fails to take into consideration, Apollo is indeed associated with dance and music; Barta 1991–92, 402.) In addition, we read about "bearded caryatids" in the novel. Male attributes of female figures offer further range to the symbol of internal division and chaos.

While Nikolai Apollonovich—who, like the other central characters, suffers from a divided consciousness—is looking at the caryatid, his legs go numb. Immobile, he resembles the mythological dancers turned into still grey stone: "He tried to clutch at externals: that caryatid—it was just a caryatid. . . . But no! He had never seen anything like it: it was hanging over a flame. And over there the little black house. . . . Here were his feet. No, no! Not feet but soft parts uselessly dangling here" (126). Whereas people are dehumanized, the bearded Atlas at the entrance of Apollon Apollonovich's department is endowed with human features. His three most "memorable" days relate to revolutionary shocks against the iron will of Peter the Great: Napoleon's attack against the Empire in 1812; the Decembrist uprising of 1825; and the Russian Revolution of 1905, taking place simultaneously with the novel's action. The "unhappy" Atlas, a "shadow" of the actual city, appears only in the Petersburg of the novel, however; according to Dolgopolov's evidence, no such bearded figure is to be found in the part of town where government offices were located (1977, 265). Another Atlas with goatlike, hairy legs and hooves—an architectural impossibility in Petersburg—typifies, however, the cerebral play in the novel: the Atlas figure represents a Titan, guardian of the pillars of Heaven, but the goatlike legs belong to Pan or the Satyrs, Dionysus' companions.

The internal division of characters allows Bely to make extensive use of the concept of the *Doppelgänger*. While people profess certain beliefs, they also stand as the "doubles" of their enemies who want to destroy them (Paperny 1983, 93; Szilard 1984, 604). One critic has postulated that Peter the Great creates the novel's "deep structure" from which the "surface structure," the characters—a series of doubles—are generated (Hedin 1982, 150). Peter's conflict with his predecessors, defenders of old Russian values, and his own son strikes an analogy with Chronos, whom Nikolai Apollonovich encounters in his "other space" when asleep. Chronos, as is well known in classical mythology, castrated his father and wanted to annihilate his children by eating them. He, in turn, was later displaced by Zeus. The figure of Peter, then, contains all opposing energies: East and West; rationalism and chaos; ruler and ruled; victim and victimizer. The architecture of the textual city reveals this "deep-structural" opposition between fathers and sons. The fictional coat of arms of the Ableukhovs captures a knight being gored by a unicorn. The knight and the unicorn, however, are each other's doubles: Apollon Apollonovich and his son, Dudkin and Lippanchenko all enact both roles (Mierau 1982, 805). The "knight," the Bronze Horseman, that is, "fathered" the city's tapering spires that resemble the horn of the unicorn (Carlson 1980, 162–63). Apollon Apollonovich is the most obvious father figure who stands for the knight, whose life is threatened. But Nikolai's life would also be threatened, if, by chance, he should refuse to kill his father. Dudkin, resembling Pushkin's Evgeny, is clearly the victim of Peter's city, yet he pierces Lippanchenko with the scissors at the Bronze Horseman's (Peter's) behest. Lippanchenko, thus, represents the knight, the gored one, but he also acts as the unicorn, the "gorer," wanting to assassinate the Senator.[5]

Each other's doubles, the two Ableukhovs share a weak will, ineffectiveness, and an essentially gentle disposition. These qualities set them apart from the aggressive powers they represent: official authority and the secret organization, respectively. Nikolai, the novel's most important character, is not only a double, a victim, and a victimizer of his father—qualities inherent in Peter the Great—but also a caricature of the city's founder, a marionette. Having found out about his mother's unexpected arrival, even as he is contemplating parricide, he finds that "[a]ll the mirrors burst into laughter, because the mirror that looked from the drawing room into the hall now reflected a Petrushka" (154). Not only is Petrushka a popular figure in Russia, debunking official ideology in the carnival of the marketplace, but the name is also the diminutive of Peter. That name in the Russian consciousness and, in particular, in this novel, signifies the greatest and most controversial tsar.

Reflection and doubling also mark the city's architecture. Peter the Great's attempts to copy Dutch, French, and German urban planning produced a definite pattern for the Russian capital. Western-looking blocks line the streets all over the city, not just in the affluent center, but in the less fashionable, sometimes squalid, islands and the outskirts too. The buildings are as ambiguous as the tsar who had them designed. Readers of *Crime and Punishment* will recall how the orderly, decorated, neoclassical facades hide quintessential Russian misery. When many outlying areas were built in the eighteenth century under the reigns of Anna, Elizabeth, and Catherine the Great, wooden constructions, onion domes, and other traditional ingredients of Russian architecture were prohibited (Berman 1982, 179). But the space behind the outer walls of buildings, in the best spirit of the Patyomkin village, concerned no one. When the young muzhik, Stepka, arrives at the home of his old friend, now a caretaker on Vasilievsky Island, the lower-class "idyll" that meets him seems familiar to the reader of nineteenth-century Russian prose by such writers as Gogol or Dostoevsky: "The door squealed, and the porter, Morzhov, raised his head. His fat sloppy wife (she always had an earache) had piled up plump pillows and had spent the day exterminating bedbugs" (66).

Urban poverty and ugly factories in the outskirts also belong to the Western aspects of St. Petersburg, whose major industrial sites resemble their English or French prototypes. When the peasant lad is approaching the capital on foot from the country in search of employment, he sees no redeeming features as he casts his glance on the black ring of factories surrounding the city: "A road winds from Kolpino: there is no gloomier spot! . . . There a workman was plodding along . . . he was hoofing it to Petersburg. . . . Squatting behind chimneys were factories—here, there and everywhere. In the sky there was no trace of a cloud, and everywhere the horizon was choking with soot. And noxious cinders dirtied everything. And chimneys bristled against the cinders" (66).

The young peasant has to transcend the spatial boundary between the Russian countryside and the westernized city. The concept of such borderlines as those between East and West, Russia and Europe, the visible and the invisible city, preoccupies the novel throughout. As Nikolai Apollonovich and Dudkin are walking along the street, they agree that they cannot really establish the ontological nature of anything. They look into shop windows where they see reflections. Things appear to be themselves and yet not quite themselves: "'... everything's real, yet not quite real. ... Look: this shop window—there are reflections in the window, there's a gentleman going by—look: there we are, you see? Yet it's somehow strange....' 'Or consider this: objects ... the devil only knows *what* they are. Real yet not quite real...'"(183; italics in the original).

Even the format of the printed page hints at irrational encounters between creatures of different spatial and temporal dimensions in *Petersburg*. The text contains an extensive number of typographical intrusions: we come across indented passages that appear to serve no semantic purpose. The typographical layout indicates intrusions into the text comparable to the transcendent forcing itself into the human mind. Nearly half the intrusions treat the subject of the bomb, which represents the "transcendent" (Alexandrov 1985, 124). These intrusions create an effect as sudden and unexplained as the unexpected interruptions in the narration. A boat keeps appearing and disappearing on the canals; at other times, a red, illuminated carriage rushes past the walkers. The narrating voice remains cryptic about the nature or function of these occurrences: "Likhutin moaned and shook his head, feeling his brain working very keenly, while reflections crept over the walls: a small steamboat was going by on the Moika, leaving bright bands of light on the waters" (133).

The seemingly harmoniously enclosed family scene in the Ableukhov house after the mother's return offers the chance for the last conversation to take place between father and son, which reminds both of them of happier days in the past. And suddenly, the whistle of a boat outside slightly marrs the brief accord inside. Vessels on the city's waterways inevitably call to mind the myth of Petersburg. Tsar Peter, with Western-European technology, attempted to subdue hostile "elements": various forms of water as well as human resistance. But the "elements" will not be walled in by Peter's will.

The latter haunts the city. Apart from Falconet's statue, the Bronze Horseman, the carriage and the boat also indicate his presence. While the "Flying Dutchman," Peter, that is, sails past five times in the narrative, he remains unconnected to the characters. But in the mythological, rather than historical, time that prevails in *Petersburg*, no event stays unrelated to Peter. The mythological figure of the tsar intrudes into the plot when characters encounter existential challenges. On the ominous night when the double agent threatens both Ableukhovs, Dudkin is visited by the Bronze Horseman. Apollon Apollonovich also hears the hoofbeat of an approaching horseman, a motif consistently identified with Peter. He has just been told about plans to assassinate him. After Nikolai has been offered the choice of carrying out the assassination, committing suicide, or being arrested by the police, he "sees" Peter at a tavern later that night.

The text clearly attempts to expose the coexistence of different times and spaces within a fourth dimension. In his occult experience, Dudkin's otherworldly visitor, Shishnarfne, explains how different realms coexist and demonstrates how "easy" the transition from one to the other is: "He had leaned against the window and had become a contour (or, two-dimensional), had become a thin layer of soot of the sort you knock out of a lamp. Now this black soot had suddenly smoldered away into an ash that gleamed in the moonlight, and the ash was flying away. And there was no contour" (207). Such a metamorphosis symbolizes that nothing is what it seems and that "higher realities" are masked by everyday appearances. The city's walkers constantly encounter boundaries and the possibility of crossing them. The river and its many canals present the most prominent physical line of division in Petersburg. The dark waters, like enormous and mysterious mirrors, reveal dim two-dimensional images of the city and its inhabitants. Frequently, impenetrable fog envelops the black bridges across the Neva. The narrating persona sees "Manchurian caps" crossing the bridges, clearly implying "penetration" from East to West (note that Sofia Petrovna's Japanese decoration at her home and the oriental atmosphere surrounding Nikolai Ableukhov also bear witness to the spread of the "Eastern spirit"). The caps belong to Russian soldiers who returned from the Russo-Japanese war "infected" by "Panmongolism" (Steinberg 1978, 528).

Bridges connect the glittering central area, housing the government, with the dark, foggy islands where civil disobedience sustains the secret organization. But double agents cross the bridges and ensure that each entity penetrates the other. Spies, the most "transitional" walkers, benefit greatly from the opportunity to disappear easily in this city of shadows. The double agent, called at certain times Morkovin and Voronkov at others, appears "dissected" into a nose and an enormous wart. His top hat is seen crossing the river and disappearing in the fog throughout the novel; this is hardly surprising since he occupies a residence on Nevsky Prospect in his capacity as a government informer and one on Vasilevsky Island as a spy, working for the "party."

The river reminds Nikolai of divisions as he walks down the Moika listening to threats from the double agent, "Morkovin-Voronkov": "The Neva opened out. Here was the stone curve of the Winter Canal; here the wind made its onslaughts. And beyond the Neva rose the outlines of islands and houses; and they cast their amber eyes into their mists; and they seemed to be weeping" (141). None of the characters suffers more from being torn between contradictory forces than Nikolai Apollonovich. Unintentionally, he belongs both to the "party" and the government: to the former by his own careless promise, motivated by a sudden surge of hatred prompting him to kill his father, and to the latter simply by living in his aristocratic home as the son of Apollon Apollonovich. Nikolai feels that he belongs to neither group. His many walks across bridges symbolize his restless movement between two ideologically divided worlds. He made his promise to assassinate his father on a bridge; he appears before Sofia Likhutina as the Red Domino on a bridge; finally, he contemplates suicide on the bridge (Doležel 1979, 467).

Walls, staircases, doors, gates, and windows, like bridges, connect the realms of the known with the unknown. Walls, one critic argues, are like a permeable second skin in *Petersburg* (Klotz 1969, 285). It is worth noting the intertextual link with Pushkin's "Bronze Horseman," where the narrating persona comments on Peter's achievement of the city's creation:

> By nature we are fated
> To cut a window through to Europe,
> To stand with a firm foothold on the sea.
> (Pushkin 1982, 247)

The image of cutting a window has violent implications. Once it has been forced into its place on the marshes, the window, the city, that is, stands between indigenous Russians and the West. The window allows light into the house; according to Petrine intentions, European rationality and reason illuminate Russia's backwardness. But Pushkin's image also suggests that the window destroys privacy and intimacy by letting outsiders see what is happening inside. Lack of privacy, moreover, turns into a delusion the hope of instituting Western individualism. Bely's essay, "The City," illustrates this point: "Somebody is running after somebody else. A car, a bicycle, policemen are flying past. Bang—the car breached the wall, went through the room, where domestic life was peacefully running its course—bang; the car reached the wall and quietly rolled along the street. Funny, isn't it? Walls do not protect us from the coming of the invisible. A peaceful life. Funny, isn't it?" (Quoted from Tsivyan 1984, 113–14; my translation). Of course, the violent, futuristic image of a car crashing into and driving through a room inside a building completely contradicts the idea of "peaceful domestic life." The irony underlines the impossibility of sealing off ideas from the surrounding reality of Petersburg, which in itself is an odd mixture of Europe, Russia, and Asia, the world of politics, and the realm of the irrational.[6] Furthermore, no wall can protect from the fourth dimension, as Shishnarfne explains: "Petersburg is in the fourth dimension which is not indicated on maps, which is indicated merely by a dot. And this dot is the place where the plane of being is tangential to the surface of the sphere and the immense astral cosmos. A dot which in the twinkling of an eye can produce for us an inhabitant of the fourth dimension, from whom not even a wall can protect us. A moment ago I was one of the dots by the window sill, but now I have appeared" (207). According to Bely's occult knowledge, the "fourth dimension" is not occupied by people but by "all the thoughts, feelings, fears, desires, wishes, and impulses human beings feel" (Carlson 1993, 201). If the city is indeed in the "fourth dimension," it recognizes no distinction between present and past. In its architecture, the past exists in the present, as the "bearded caryatid" illustrates. Time, in other words, manifests itself spatially (Waszink 1988, 264). In Uspensky's *Tertium Organum*, an inhabitant of a two-dimensional world is believed initially to sense the existence of a third dimension as time. By gaining awareness of a third dimension, the two-dimensional creatures realize that their existence is either a mere illusion or that they have a third dimension, of which they were not conscious (Henderson 1983, 250). The attempt of doors, walls, and windows to seal a three-dimensional world in *Petersburg* is doomed because the physical world is represented as merely the shadow of a supposedly higher reality. Oppositions coexist in the higher order where cerebral play originates: The final words of Shishnarfne, the Persian ghost, "I destroy irrevocably" (208), echo the Bronze Horseman's chilling comment, "I doom: irrevocably!" (149).

In an environment like this, it makes no difference whether one is inside walls or outside in the street. Apollon Apollonovich senses hostility radiating towards him on his walk: "It now seemed to him that even that stupid wall hated him" (*Peterburg* 198). "The chief benefit of the house,"—according to Bachelard—is that it "shelters daydreaming, protects the dreamer, and allows one to dream in peace." "Onto what, towards what do doors open?"—he asks, and concludes with a quotation from Ramon Gomez de la Serna: "Doors that open on the countryside seem to confer freedom behind the world's back" (1964, 224). Doors in *Petersburg* open onto a hostile world: "The tinkle of the doorbell was heard, surely, someone uninvited was giving a reminder of his existence; he wanted to come in here from the grey, wicked fog and from the slush of the street, but nobody responded to his request. And then again the doorbell rang sharply. Surely someone started crying. There the entrance door to the hall banged questioningly and when the void was wide enough between the walls and the door, a little black mask carefully thrust its nose in from the emptiness" (*Peterburg* 156). While, on the one hand, the narrating voice relates that children are awaiting the arrival of people wearing masks, on the other hand, an undeniable tone of existential fear prevails. The door "banged questioningly": those inside seem unsure about who wants to enter and why, and whoever is knocking outside does not know what awaits him indoors even if he should be admitted. Bearing in mind that the scene takes place at the ball where one of the guests is the "Red Domino," anxiety concerning the identity of the uninvited intruder establishes an intertextual link with Edgar Allen Poe's "Mask of the Red Death." The idea of the "unexpected" preoccupies the consciousness of the entire text. At one point, the narrating voice addresses the reader directly: "'Suddenlys' are familiar to you. Why, then, do you bury your head like an ostrich at the approach of the inexorable 'suddenly'? 'It' sneaks up behind your back. Sometimes it even precedes your appearance in a room. You feel horribly uneasy. In your back grows the sensation that a gang of things invisible has shoved its way in through a door. You turn, you ask your hostess: 'Madam, would you mind if I close the door? I can't bear to sit with my back to the door'" (23). Dudkin, the Likhutins, and Anna Petrovna all seem to have frightening experiences with doors. The Ableukhovs dislike walking, partially because they fear what awaits them behind doors. The phenomenology of the door contains the threat of the unexpected violation of the civilizing force that ensures the intimacy of sealed-off space.

Attempts to break through symbolize a desire to destroy divisions. Architecturally, the factory chimneys, turrets, domes, and spires all break through the fog, uniting the sunny sky with the muggy mist below (Woronzoff 1982, 54). Piercing and drilling also unite, albeit in a rather radical manner. It was discussed earlier that the piercing horn of the unicorn and its victim, the knight, symbolize the violent struggle between the people of *Petersburg*. But, while the union is violent, it puts an end to animosity, as is illustrated by the image of Dudkin, in the pose of the Bronze Horseman, when he has mounted the corpse of his victim and victimizer, Lippanchenko: "[T]here was a corpse; and a small figure, with a laughing white face. It had a small moustache, with bristling ends. How strange: the man had mounted the dead body. In his hands he was clutching a pair of scissors" (264). Dudkin used a pair of scissors as his murder weapon. Nikolai Apollonovich thinks of using a pair of scissors against his father. Piercing weapons decorate the walls of the Ableukhov house. Their owner, the Senator, wants to drill a hole in the wall between his room and his son's to be able to watch him.[7] Clearly, the bomb embodies with eloquence the attempt in *Petersburg* to end tension and opposition and to bring down walls. It is typical of the futility of the novel's feverish undertakings that the bomb largely fails in its mission.

The novel's form, complete with a prologue, an epilogue, mottoes preceding chapters, and the final words "The End," looks like a genre-parody, evoking the mannerisms of eighteenth-century neoclassicism. The traditional framework, however, contradicts the fragmented, modernist text, in which unexpected indented passages appear and we find highly unusual punctuation. The contrast has its analogy in the city's plurality: geometrically ordered, classical architecture coexists with an irrational and unpredictable world of gloomy, wet backstreets and the poverty of inner yards and staircases. Bely's characters must constantly be on the go, haunted and unsafe in Peter's city, and the readers also need to keep wandering about the text, rushing back or dashing ahead, if they want to make sense and unfold the secrets of *Petersburg*.

CHAPTER 3

Ulysses
The City of the Wandering Aengus and the Wandering Jew

Petersburg is the final and greatest literary evocation of the Russian capital before the Bolshevik revolution of 1917. Ulysses is the first and still unrivaled novelistic depiction of Dublin before Irish independence from Britain. Written almost simultaneously and published within six years of each other (Ulysses appeared in 1922), both works mediate experiences of their city's reality in highly innovative narratives: in addition to the fabric of life, the two writers utilize the linguistic and literary cultures of the two capitals in their novels. In these modernist texts, the city combines the roles of protagonist and coauthor. Without Dublin, Ulysses and Finnegans Wake could not have been written and the same holds true for the relationship between St. Petersburg and Bely's novel.

No wonder that even Bely's contemporaries referred to him as the "Russian Joyce" (Zamyatin 1970, 242, 245). It has long intrigued Bely scholars whether the two men knew each other or were familiar with each other's work. Joyce and Bely may very well have lived in Switzerland contemporaneously during World War I; furthermore, it also appears more than likely that Bely saw an edition of, or at least heard of, Ulysses in Berlin or later in Moscow, where a fragment of Joyce's novel appeared in Russian translation (Tall 1984). The evidence available to us regarding possible links between the two men, however, remains nebulous: Beckett attended a lecture on Bely in Dresden in 1937 and may have discussed it with Joyce; George Reavey may have spoken to Joyce about Bely in Paris (Cornwell 1989, 45).

Students and scholars of Joyce are largely unaware of Bely. The term "Russian Joyce" bespeaks a Russian sense of inferiority vis à vis Western culture that the isolationist tendencies of communist rule under the Soviets exacerbated. Even if Joyce and Bely had read each other, it is far from certain that they would have been favorably impressed. The relationship between the two texts lies outside the vague areas of literary influence and biographical similarities.

While the Russian capital appears with some topographical accuracy in Bely's novel, an intentional lack of identity between the geographical and fictional cities reminds us of the presence of the powerful symbolism elaborated in the urban imagery. The objects of the physical world realize ideas and serve as points of departure for retreats into inner worlds. *Ulysses*, strangely enough, has less symbolic power invested in its title than Bely's *Petersburg*, nor is the city of Dublin primarily a symbol in the novel. The Homeric metaphor exerts control over the development of the narrative and assists readers in following the complex trajectories of characters. The Dublin of the novel preserves a strong sense of the freshness of reality: such minor changes as Joyce's calling the church in "Lotus Eaters" "All Hallows" instead of the accurate "St. Andrew's" do not alter this (Nicholson 1988, 60). Within his frame of reference, Joyce creates the effect of verisimilitude in the evocation of the city by cleverly mixing the real with the fictional. He once suggested that were Dublin to disappear, it could be reconstructed from *Ulysses*, and that the novel was a verbal representation of the city (Hart and Knuth 1975, 13). But were we to return to the Dublin of 1904 in a time capsule, we would find no Leopold or Molly Bloom living in 7 Eccles Street; the house stood unoccupied at the time of the novel and now it no longer exists. Nor could Nighttown be recreated on the basis of the "Circe" chapter either (Benstock 1972, 101).

By the time he started work on the novel, Joyce had left Ireland forever. Besides his vivid memories of the Irish capital, he corresponded with his aunt, Josephine Murray, who lived in Dublin, and with his brother Stanislaus, who knew the city well, even though he was in residence in Trieste during all the years *Ulysses* was being written. These two people could confirm the accuracy of Joyce's recollection of details. He also used Thom's Dublin Directory to ensure credibility in the literary evocation of the city. While the main characters are fictitious, we can locate thirty of the minor characters in Thom's Directory (Ellmann 1982, 357–79, and Kain 1947, 121). Matching Bely's fascination with St. Petersburg, Joyce regarded Dublin as a unique place in the world. He said: "The expression 'Dubliner' seems to me to bear some meaning and I doubt whether the same can be said for such words as 'Londoner' or 'Parisian,' both of which have been used by authors as titles" (quoted from Gorman 1939, 146).

Perched on the eastern and western edges of Europe, the St. Petersburg and Dublin of Joyce's and Bely's novels capture the experience of modern urban life and civilization with greater vividness than textual representations of more prominent mainland European cities do. Although the Russian imperial capital was built as late as the eighteenth century, Dublin has been a capital city for almost two thousand years. Yet both the physical and intellectual aspects of these cities show analogous features. In the eighteenth century,

Dublin, like Petersburg, became the second largest city in its country. Bisected by rivers that merge into the sea, both Dublin and St. Petersburg are dominated by graceful, neoclassical buildings in the central areas. Custom House, the Bank of Ireland, Trinity College, and the Four Courts Building contrasted sharply with the squalid, narrow streets of tenement houses at the beginning of the twentieth century.

The events in *Ulysses* take place in Dublin in 1904 when the city was relatively small, with a population between three and four hundred thousand. Joyce shuns the industrial side of his city and focuses on the commercial, intellectual, and religious features of the Irish capital in whose "walkable" center on the two sides of the Liffey many of the characters of *Ulysses* know each other and keep meeting. While Petersburg in 1905 has its fair quota of automobiles, only one appears in *Ulysses*; lack of engine noise makes it easier for people to chat in the street (Nicholson 1988, viii). In Bely's *Petersburg*, social and political divisions seem secondary to the spiritual aspects of the city; commerce and industry in the Russian capital are all but neglected in the text. Readers of the novels will not fully appreciate that Dublin and St. Petersburg contained some of Europe's worst slums at the time.

Both cities also appeared incongruous within their countries. Just as the Russian city's "rectilinear" and "European" character, aspiring toward a capitalist economic structure, was perceived as alien in half-feudal, agricultural, and provincial Russia, Dublin—an increasingly industrial city in an undeveloped rural Ireland with few large towns—was regarded as decidedly foreign. As a strong reminder of the proximity of rustic Ireland proper, we see a herd of cattle driven to the docks in Joyce's Dublin when in the "Hades" chapter the funeral cortege has to let the animals go past at the corner of Berkeley Road and the North Circular Road. Many people would say even today that modern Dublin does not really represent the rest of Ireland. In 1904, and even today to a lesser extent, Dublin was thoroughly rooted in British traditions and, of course, the English language and culture. From a British perspective, Dublin was the "Queen City of the Empire" (Dumbleton 1984, 149). The many Irish nationalists, however, wanted to see Dublin become the administrative and political center of an independent republic, and they considered English, ironically their own mother tongue, as the language of their oppressors. It is precisely because of such contradictions that a relatively small and marginal city like Joyce's Dublin can embody the modern experience in greater depth than Dos Passos' New York, Farrell's Chicago, or Woolf's London (Benstock 1972, 83).

Ulysses is the twentieth-century novel of walking *par excellence*. While it depicts aspects of Dublin with microscopic precision, *Ulysses* uncovers the inner world of the city's walkers in far more detail than *Petersburg*. The duration of events in the plot amounts to fewer than twenty-four hours. Apart from the four chapters that take place largely inside the home—"Telemachos," "Calypso," "Ithaca" and "Penelope"—the story traces the wanderings of the two protagonists, Leopold Bloom and Stephen Dedalus: the narrative accounts for Bloom's movements almost comprehensively from 8 o'clock in the morning on 16 June 1904 until about 2 o'clock the next morning. Stephen's afternoon wanderings slow down as he spends some six hours drinking in various pubs; the coverage of his movements is not absolutely complete at this period. Bloom performs a circular movement, leaving his house in 7 Eccles Street and returning to it at the end of his day. Stephen's "return" remains incomplete: he fails to go back to the martello tower where his day started, nor does he stay at Bloom's in Eccles Street. As the two men ramble about, they frequently stop at a variety of places, on business, out of a sense of duty, for fun, or from simply having nothing better to do. Bloom covers about eighteen miles: eight on foot and some ten by tram, horse-drawn carriage, and train (Nicholson 1988, vii). Stephen also speeds up his progress, occasionally taking the tram and the train.

The surnames Bloom and Dedalus are metaphorical and suggest wandering. Daedalus, the legendary artisan, had a significant name: "daidala" in ancient Greek means "artful works." He spent his life wandering from place to place. He created an artifact, the labyrinth, and then made himself wings to escape from Crete; analogously, Joyce created the labyrinth of *Ulysses* and both of his semiautobiographical heroes, Bloom and Stephen, dream about freeing themselves and escaping. The name "Bloom" is the English translation of the original Hungarian surname, Virág, which used to belong to Bloom's ancestor, an immigrant to Ireland. As a common noun, "virág" means "flower" in Hungarian. The family was Jewish: better-off Jewish people in the Habsburg empire could buy themselves mellifluous German names, such as Rosenfeld, Rosenberger, or for that matter, Blum or Blume. "Blum"—a common enough Jewish name—means flower in German, and "Virág," by all likelihood, is its Magyarized variant. In fact, the name itself contains the history of the "Wandering Jew."

Wandering in the mind constantly accompanies physical walking. The shared space of Dublin does not prevent characters from sealing themselves off in their own individual time-space. However, all movement, mental and physical alike, takes place in a narrative.

In *Petersburg* we saw a narrator-function; several voices mediated the characters' various physical/spiritual experiences, some establishing ironical distance, others—close to the intended intellectual center of the text—using high-flown rhetoric. First-person narration, addressing the reader, suggests the author's presence in his textual city. The author of *Ulysses* is not, however, to be seen walking around in his Dublin. Like Stephen's Shakespeare, he is not absent from, but hidden by, the novel: "[Shakespeare] goes back, weary of the creation he has piled up to hide him from himself, an old dog licking an old sore" (9.474–76).[1] The author plays a game of hide-and-seek in his text. The text itself behaves toward its reader rather like the city does toward its walkers: the narration contains thousands of clues, helpful and misleading ones alike, that serve as so many hints to the reader-navigator. The reader finds him/herself compelled to become Odysseus (Thomas 1982, 1 and 37). In a letter to Harriet Shaw Weaver, written on 25 February 1920, Joyce clearly suggested that he considered the acts both of writing and of reading the novel as "odysseys." In the manner of Homer and Shakespeare, Joyce is a writer of "negative capability," a term coined by John Keats referring to writing without moralizing or revealing personal attitudes. The "god-author," like an Olympian, helps and hinders the characters, as he creates them and their wanderings. The title *Ulysses* metaphorically alludes to a larger pattern than the Homeric epic generates: movement about town, at least in Bloom's case, is "homebound," ending in his return to Molly, who awaits him in her bed. The reader wanders with some confusion as the narrative perspective, disguised by a broad variety of stylistic devices, keeps changing. This technique creates an effect similar to that of the film montage which Bely and, in particular, Döblin, also use effectively. As Joyce constructs meandering paths for his readers amidst which they face the perils of getting lost or, worse still, getting out by abandoning the book altogether, he builds a Dublin of words. Thus, he accomplishes his own *nostos* to the city that he left for a self-imposed exile. The subscript at the end of the text,

"Trieste-Zurich-Paris
1914–1921," (18.1610–11)

captures the wanderings of Joyce himself while he was working on his *Ulysses*. Bely achieves the same effect in creating his fictional city, which, while presented as a symbol more explicitly than Joyce's, still evokes Petersburg more powerfully than did the work of any of his predecessors, including such writers as Gogol, Dostoevsky, and Tolstoy. Joyce, of course, does not write against a constricting ideological grid like Bely but his characters are, ironically, oblivious to the Homeric parallels, just as characters in *Petersburg* are mostly unaware of the cerebral play responsible for their existence (Barta 1988, 1147). Both Bely and Joyce reject the positivist depiction of reality in the manner of classic realist mimesis. Bely "reflects" the mind's image of the city and Joyce's shifting perspectives create "self-reflecting mirror effects" (Thomas 1982, 50). The viewpoints in *Ulysses* are integrated into the plot: the merging of "form" and "content" is complete in such chapters as "Nausicaa" where the narrator is part of Gerty MacDowell's fantasy world, or in "Cyclops" where the "narrator" turns into one of the customers at Barney Kiernan's pub.

Ulysses has no central narrator, but each narrating voice becomes part of an elaborate mosaic. By contrast, the voices of narration show a definite hierarchy in *Petersburg*; in Joyce's text not only does the narrative lack unity and any kind of hierarchy but, in addition, it fails to hint at ways of rationalizing and abridging gaps. An omniscient, organizing intelligence gives way to a broad, metonymically arranged canvas of juxtaposed segments. The narrator of "Wandering Rocks," for example, sees all movements from his vantage point above the city, but he reveals no knowledge of the walkers' inner lives (French 1976, 171). Other narrative voices, however, are privy to the workings of the mind and know the interior and exterior locations in the city, but they lack a full view of the network of movements in the novel. Moreover, the extensive use of interior monologue and stream of consciousness points to the trend within the novel's discontinuous narrative toward the inner worlds of characters. Yet, as each character moves along her or his temporal corridor, no single mind is in control. No overseeing narrator arranges the data gained from juxtaposing the many types of internal consciousness on this June day in Dublin in 1904 (Alter 1975, 141). The author has planned his universe, however: all voices exist thanks to his agency and he reserves the right to establish metaphorical relationships within the haphazard contiguity of city particles.

Each episode captures a different part of the city; only "Calypso," "Ithaca," and "Penelope" take place in 7 Eccles Street. The narrative techniques in each chapter explore the consciousness of the main characters.

Simultaneous movement about central Dublin appears on the broad spatial canvas of "Wandering Rocks." All the characters woven into the novel's plot up to this point appear before the eyes of an "overhead" narrator; we even see some characters walking about who will enter the story in succeeding chapters. It appears that the whole city is in the streets. While in Bely's Petersburg people rush about in a frenzied state, Joyce's Dubliners make very leisurely walkers, sauntering along the streets and stopping for generous breaks in pubs. The weather is fair on this day in Dublin, warm and sunny, unlike the dark, slushy October in Petersburg or the constantly unpleasant weather in *Berlin Alexanderplatz*. As opposed to Russia in 1905 or Germany in the late twenties, 1904 is a relatively peaceful, inactive period in the history of Ireland. *Ulysses* clearly does not aim at examining what was accomplished on this day, but instead, the novel focuses on how things are achieved. Eighteen hours on such an uneventful day as 16 June 1904 in the history of a city or in the lives of the majority of its inhabitants might well be considered quite insignificant. In the novel's consciousness, however, it is the manner in which actions happen that takes precedence over the actions themselves. Who strolls, and why, matters a great deal indeed.

The walkers with plenty of time to spare in *Ulysses* are men. The few female pedestrians in the streets of Joyce's Dublin are not there for leisure. Strolling for women was socially not fully acceptable; the fact that there were no public toilets for females is an example of the city's lack of accommodation for women who were out and about (Nicholson 1988, ix). As in Homeric society, women in *Ulysses* spend the day at home: they try to run the house without the money that flows out of their husbands' and fathers' hands in Dublin's numerous drinking establishments. Stephen's sister, Dilly Dedalus, goes out to meet her father to get some money for the survival of the family. Her sister tries and fails to sell some old books at M'Guiness' for a few badly needed pennies. If women walk about town, they pursue a husband, brother, or father who has been unsuccessful in accomplishing his task or proved incapable of managing his affairs (S. Benstock 1988, 296). Mrs. Breen is trying to catch up with her mentally incapacitated husband to take care of him; she actually saves him from being run over in "Wandering Rocks." Gerty MacDowell's bedridden father has her deliver the "Catesby's cork lino letters" (10. 1207): on her way she stops to watch the viceroy passing by. We also see some working women at the service of male customers, like the barmaids, Miss Kennedy and Miss Douce, in the Ormond Hotel or the prostitutes in "Circe."

Stephen's epiphanic fragment about Dublin life, the "Parable of Plums," captures two elderly women on an outing to Nelson's column. However, even at a moment when they are not serving the male establishment, their leisurely activity reflects their sexual, religious, and political enslavement (Ahearn 1989, 115). The two unmarried women climb the tall, "phallic," column to eat their plums. It is only from the top of a memorial of an English Protestant sailor that they can obtain a good view of their Irish Catholic city.

Domestic preoccupations keep the widowed Mrs. Dignam at home: she needs to mind her little children. Mina Purefoy is laid up in hospital, giving birth to her ninth child. But the novel's most interesting female nonwalker is Molly Bloom. At night, in bed, she mentally strolls around, envisaging some fifty places in and around Dublin, in addition to the Gibraltar locations of her childhood (McCarthy 1986, 78). She has nowhere to go from her home in Eccles Street. She is a sidelined singer who has not given a concert for more than a year. She appears to have no friends to visit and her one responsibility for the day, supervising her charwoman, keeps her indoors. She looks forward to a big event, an amorous encounter to take place in the house with Blazes Boylan, originally a professional acquaintance. In gossipy Dublin, Molly could not have such a liaison outside her own house.

The social mores that assign women their space in the city account, at least partially, for the sour atmosphere in the home. Intellectually, and often financially, frustrated, women channel their ambitions into a rigid and hapless domestic order from which men prefer to flee, favoring the liberation and socializing the city can offer (S. Benstock 1988, 301). The central event for the many male characters on 16 June is Paddy Dignam's funeral. None of them seems to be a particularly close friend of the deceased and yet they would not miss the sad event for anything: they have no problem making time to go to the funeral. Relaxed strolling about the streets, with frequent stops for drinks, follows the burial service. Simon Dedalus, Stephen's father, goes to "The Oval" with Ned Lambert from the cemetery; after closing time in midafternoon, he wanders over to the Ormond Hotel where, in all likelihood, he will sing, muse, drink, and natter away before returning to his near-starving children in 7 St. Peter's Terrace late in the evening. Patrick Aloysius Dignam, the deceased man's son, prefers to avoid the home of his mourning siblings and his widowed mother: he goes two miles from their house to Mangan's butcher's shop to buy one and a half pounds of pork steaks for his mother. Surely he could easily have bought the meat nearer his home had he not wanted to kill time.

The opportunity and desire of men in Dublin to potter around and gossip clearly intrigued Joyce. He said, "I wonder if there is another [city] like it. Everybody has time to hail a friend and start a conversation about a third party" (quoted from Budgen 1937, 60). Joyce's Dublin in 1904 is made for that intriguing creature of the European metropolis of the age, the mixture of the flâneur and the badaud. People have time on their hands: they do not seem to have full-time jobs, nor have they particularly pleasant and welcoming homes to return to. A broad range of verbs denotes the activity of walking about in *Ulysses*: in addition to walking, characters cakewalk, doubleshuffle, keel row, galliard, and mazurka around town (Long 1982, 152); in "Lotus Eaters," Bloom strolls, saunters, wanders, lolls, and halts. Lenehan—well-known to readers of the "Two Gallants"—is a footloose wanderer who walks in circles thrice around the city in *Dubliners*. In *Ulysses*, a desire to socialize and kill time explains his choice of route from Crampton Court to the Ormond Hotel in the "Wandering Rocks" chapter. Lenehan is going to meet Boylan there but has plenty of time before the meeting. His walking companion is M'Coy. Instead of going out to Essex Street and then straight to the Ormond Quay, crossing the Liffey on Grattan Bridge, they wander along to Temple Bar—quite the opposite direction from the Ormond Hotel—walk under Merchants' Arch to the river where they turn left to reach finally Grattan Bridge, where the two part company and Lenehan enters the hotel on his own in the "Sirens" chapter.

For the most part, it is sexual pursuits that motivate the wanderings of the Dublin *bon vivant*, Blazes Boylan. Bloom alone sees him three times in the street, and the reader encounters him more frequently still. A man of leisure, he casually rings his secretary, Miss Dunne, to sort out his business matters, as he is buying pears and peaches at Thornton's fruit and flower shop. At the bottom of the hamper he has port and potted meat that, complete with the fruit, he sends ahead to Molly, who sits at home waiting for him as he strolls, shops, and womanizes on this cheerful day.

The sunny Dublin of *Ulysses* is the same place as the city suffering from paralysis and lack of vision in *Dubliners*. Amidst the constant chatter of the strolling Dubliners, little gets accomplished and an impression of futility and wasted opportunities arises: the piano tuner—a blind stripling—spends long hours reaching places to earn his living. Having tuned the piano at the Ormond Hotel, he leaves his tuning fork behind to have to tap his way back later from S. Frederick Street to retrieve the instrument. The begging, one-legged sailor slowly going from Gardiner Street toward Nelson Street, via Dorset Street and Eccles Street, creates a distressing image of a wasted life. The two women in the "Parable of Plums" embody futility: they spend their savings buying plums to quench their thirst after eating their impoverished meal of brawn. On top of Nelson's column, they feel dizzy looking down and they suffer from a cramp in their neck when they look up, so they finally end up doing neither (Nicholson 1988, 92). Throughout the day, walkers of *Ulysses* keep seeing five sandwichmen advertising "Hely's"; in a formation, each carries one of the letters to create an image of a walking word in the center of Dublin. Strolling up and down Grafton Street, Westmoreland Street, then across the river, and along Sackville Street, seems to be all they do. Finally, the Breens waste the day by going from one solicitor to another at the behest of the deranged husband who wants to file a libel suit for receiving an anonymous postcard, reading "U. P.: up."

All these characters in the city's streets owe their existence in the novel to their position around the two most important walkers, Stephen and Bloom. Primarily it is their "homeless" and dispossessed status that connects these two characters. They have no alternative to spending their day walking about Dublin. If they were in a hurry, they could go about by tram, but they rarely choose to do so. They have hardly any urgent business to attend to. Their predominant wish is to be away from home. Buck Mulligan has taken away Stephen's key to the martello tower, but Stephen has no intention of returning there anyway. Bloom has left his key at home in the morning, which is just as well: he has no wish to return to his house because he suspects that his wife is going to receive her lover in their bedroom during the course of the day.

Both Bloom and Stephen feel uncomfortable in Dublin, where their fellow citizens reject them. While born and raised as an Irishman, his being half-Jewish and of foreign descent makes other Dubliners consider Bloom an "outsider," not quite one of them. He knows a great number of people, but he has no close friend. While many of the men in the numerous pubs are on a first-name basis with each other, nobody calls Bloom by his first name. An artistic and nonconformist young man, Stephen also feels unwanted in the city. He had been living in Paris until he was summoned home to his dying mother. After returning from the cosmopolitan, liberated, and artistically sophisticated world of Paris to backward, provincial, and intolerant Dublin, Stephen feels profoundly out of place.

Joyce was familiar with this sense of homelessness and rejection in his own city. In a letter, he once wrote to Nora Barnacle, his future wife: "I have wandered like a mongrel dog that has received a lash across the eyes . . . [that] wandered about the streets like some filthy cur whose mistress had cut him with her whip and hunted him from her door" (Joyce 1966, 2.265–66). The image of the abused dog keeps recurring in the novel. In "Proteus," Stephen sees the "bloated carcass of a dog" (3.286). In the meantime, another dog is approaching, out on a walk with its masters. This dog, a mongrel called Tatters, sniffs around the dead one for which, as a punishment, it gets kicked by its owner. Clearly, no one cared for the dead dog or else its body would not be rotting away on the beach. Stephen feels sorry for, and identifies with, the dead dog: "Ah, poor dogsbody! Here lies poor dogsbody's body," he muses (3.351–52). Earlier, Mulligan addresses him as "dogsbody" (1.112) and Stephen refers to himself as such (1.137). But Stephen is terrified of Tatters, wondering: "Lord, is he going to attack me?" (3.295). Tatters' conformity assures that, when dead, it will not be left abandoned and unburied. Fear of the conformists and solidarity toward, even identity with, the lonely and the forsaken characterize Stephen's own position in the world. Obsequious dogs at their masters' beck and call are portrayed as highly disagreeable in *Ulysses*. A retriever growls viciously at the end of "Circe" when the policeman, Private Carr, strikes Stephen in the face. A "mangy mongrel" (12.120), called Garryowen, belongs to the chauvinist "Citizen" in "Cyclops." A frightening dog, it terrorizes Bloom and chases the carriage on which he makes his escape from the "citizen." This is the most violent incident for Bloom during the entire day, and it most clearly illustrates his inability to be accepted as one of the Dubliners. Unlike Stephen, Bloom would actually like to conform, but they will not let him. In the dream world of "Circe" Bloom gets thrashed by the ladies for supposedly making indecent proposals. The passage contains several references likening Bloom to dogs: "mongrel," "pigdog," "pupped" (15.1102–14).

The lonely walker, the outsider—having no home to return to—alludes to the figure of Diogenes and the ancient cynics (*kynos* is ancient Greek for dog). In Joyce's own experience, writing created a feeling analogous to the Diogenes-like sense of nonbelonging. He said to a friend, Claud Sykes, that as long as he could write he could live in a tub anywhere, like Diogenes (Ellmann 1982, 110).

As Bloom and Stephen follow their itineraries, Buck Mulligan perceives a link between the two and refers to Stephen as the "wandering Aengus" (9.1093) and to Bloom as the "wandering jew" (9.1209).[2] Surrounded by the same urban space, Bloom and Stephen are in a somewhat similar predicament. In the reflections of "Ithaca," Bloom, in his desire to emphasize his bond with Stephen, suggests that even if they see things differently, it is the same things they see, albeit in a parallactic way: "Though they didn't see eye to eye in everything, a certain analogy there somehow was as if both their minds were travelling, so to speak, in the one train of thought" (16.1579–81). They follow in each other's footsteps all day; on Stephen's part unconsciously, on Bloom's part—after their meeting in the lying-in hospital in the evening—consciously. Their "peripatetic ellipses" differ notably though: a "centrifugal departer," Stephen does not complete his circle while Bloom, a "centripetal remainer," returns to his point of departure (17.1214). The two men share an incomplete harmony with each other as they walk to Bloom's house in the small hours of 17 June to have a hot cup of cocoa. Reflecting the somewhat uneasy relationship between Odysseus and Telemachus, who had little in common at the time of Odysseus' return, Bloom and Stephen interpret the surrounding world differently. Bloom typifies "metonymic consciousness"; he is more preoccupied with contiguity than analogy between items (Lodge 1977, 140). Typically, on a visit to the National Library in the "Scylla and Charybdis" chapter, Bloom looks up an advertisement in the *Kilkenny People* while Stephen on the same premises at the same time engages in a discussion about *Hamlet* and Shakespeare. Stephen tends to relate pieces of reality as he encounters them to a world of images and allusions drawn from reading rather than to the tangible world around him.

Their few responsibilities do not justify the day-long wanderings. Stephen teaches a class of literature and history in Mr. Deasy's school in Dalkey. Here he promises the headmaster to deliver his letters on foot-and-mouth disease to Mr. Crawford and Mr. Russell, newspaper editors in central Dublin. He finishes at the school at half past ten and has nothing to do until half past twelve. At that time he has an appointment with Mulligan in "The Ship," a pub in the city center, but he decides to cancel it. When he reaches Sandymount, he heads toward central Dublin on foot and begins his daylong stroll. On Sandymount strand he remembers that he really ought to go to the dentist to have his bad teeth repaired and that he needs to buy himself a handkerchief, but nothing comes of these thoughts all day.

Stephen's interior monologues suggest artistic creativity, but he does nothing particularly artistic all day: he composes a quatrain on the strand, but the piece is unintentionally plagiarized (Benstock 1985, 104). Like many other floating walkers, he verges on being an alcoholic. His father rejects him, but his own greatest fear is to become like his father as a result of genetic inheritance. He resembles his father more than he would like to admit: he spends his time and money in pubs and does nothing, just like Simon Dedalus.

Stephen feels slighted by everybody. His poems have not been included in an anthology of young Irish poets. Not he, but Buck Mulligan, the medical student, receives an invitation to a party of literary men. Even the ignorant milkwoman shows no interest in him at the martello tower in the morning: "She bows her old head to a voice that speaks to her loudly, her bonesetter, her medicineman: me she slights" (1.419–20). In the vision of "Circe," Stephen meets "Old Gummy Granny," the nighttown equivalent of the milkwoman, who would only too happily sacrifice Stephen for Ireland. "Gummy Granny"— a "grotesque version of Kathleen Ni Houlihan"—represents Irish nationalism (Nicholson 1988, 54). But Stephen feels unhappy in Ireland, and he is too powerless, too much a victim of its all-encompassing paralysis, to leave.[3]

Walking away from the known and the disliked, rejected by his friends and his father, Stephen is heading toward the unknown. Bloom, however, wants nothing so much as to consolidate his place in a familiar world. His responsibilities are few: he works as an advertisement canvasser for the *Freeman's Journal* and he needs to locate an old design in the library for an advertisement for Alexander Keyes, the tea merchant. Apart from this official assignment, he occupies himself with social matters: he attends Paddy Dignam's funeral, then visits the widow to advise her about insurance matters, and goes to the lying-in hospital where another distant acquaintance is in labor. For his own pleasure, he picks up a letter from his secret correspondent in the post office, wanders about, has a bath, eats and drinks in various pubs, masturbates on a beach, and then follows Stephen around. He goes anywhere but home. Not surprisingly, he cannot take his mind off his wife betraying him. Bumping into Boylan, the lover, from time to time, does not help matters. Such conversations in town as with M'Coy in chapter 4 or with Nosey Flynn in chapter 8 also keep reminding him of his unhappy state as a cuckolded husband. They both ask, "Who's getting it up?" with reference to Molly's concert tour in the Ulster Hall in Belfast at the end of the month (5.153; 8.773). Of course, Bloom knows very well that it is Boylan, Molly's lover, who is "getting it up" but tries to avoid mentioning his name in his responses.

Wandering about without keys like Stephen, Bloom is definitely a loner in Dublin. Odysseus is also a lonely figure, particularly in *The Iliad*. Like Bloom, Odysseus is not lacking in friends because he is uncaring; he is devoted to his family and he is a loyal leader. However, he is cleverer than his associates, who therefore mistrust him (Stanford 1968, 79). Bloom also differs from others: he prefers reasoning to bragging, does not waste his earnings on drink and, "worst" of all, his fellow citizens stigmatize him as a Jew. Gummy Granny's outbursts in "Circe," "Strangers in my house, bad manners to them" (15.4586), illustrate the type of mostly repressed hostility Bloom as a "stranger" encounters all the time. Although Bloom says to himself, "Ireland [is] my country" (7.87), he still yearns for another homeland where he is not an outsider: "Lay me in my native earth. Bit of clay from the holy land" (6.819). But the consciousness of *Ulysses* eschews sentimentality. Bloom's recurring fantasies about Israel, an eastern city, about love and warmth remind one of his professional discourse as an advertiser: "All for a woman, home and houses, silk webs, silver, rich fruits spicy from Jaffa" (8.635–36).

Stephen makes him think of what his own son, Rudy, could have been like had he lived. He follows Stephen after dark to protect him from bad company. When he first catches sight of Stephen from the funeral cortege in the morning, he starts reminiscing about Rudy: "Mr Bloom at gaze saw a lithe young man, clad in mourning, a wide hat. —There's a friend of yours gone by, Dedalus, he said. —Who is that? —Your son and heir.... If little Rudy had lived. See him grow up. Hear his voice in the house. Walking beside Molly in Eton suit. My son. Me in his eyes" (6.39–43, 6.75–76). Perhaps because both men wear mourning clothes, Bloom in fact is taken for Stephen's father in "Circe." Stephen's intellect impresses Bloom and he feels sorry for the young man. Bloom attributes his own personal misery to not having a son. If he had one like Stephen, he assumes, his family life would improve considerably. Among the people with whom he associates all day, he is conspicuous by his gentleness. In spite of Bloom's inferior education, Stephen agrees to a temporary union with him. Bloom, in turn, feels no hostility whatsoever coming from Stephen.

The relaxed pace of walking of the daytime now becomes animated for Bloom. For the first time, he has a purpose that gives him direction: he would like Stephen to come round to him, stay there, and maybe, come to love him as surrogate father. In spite of the exhausting day he has had and the fact that it is very late, Bloom attempts to strike up a lively conversation on the way to Eccles Street. Perhaps for the first time during the day, both characters feel safe.

The martello tower is an outright hostile environment for Stephen, and in effect, Bloom's home has also lost its protective quality. The twee charms of Bloom's bedroom have been defiled from Bloom's viewpoint as they have been used to welcome his wife's lover. The sheltering and sealed inner space of intimacy Gaston Bachelard discusses in his *Poetics of Space* is as much lacking in *Ulysses* as it is in *Petersburg*. As in Bely's novel, the supposed center of domestic life, the bed, has a prominent role to play. Here the day originates and here it also ends as Molly and Bloom are going to sleep; we also hear Molly's powerful monologue in bed, which, in a way, summarizes the novel.

The account of Stephen's day starts in bed. He complains to Mulligan about his unpleasant nocturnal incident with Haines, the English visitor: "—He was raving all night about a black panther. . . (1.57). —I was [in a funk], Stephen said with energy and growing fear. Out here in the dark with a man I don't know raving and moaning to himself about shooting a black panther. . . . If he stays on here I am off" (1.60–63). Stephen lives in the tower for lack of a better place, but Mulligan pays the rent on the building and makes Stephen feel increasingly unwelcome. He attempts to stir Stephen's feelings of guilt with regard to his mother's death. The awful image of his dying mother haunts Stephen with great frequency: "A bowl of white china had stood beside her deathbed holding the green sluggish bile which she had torn up from her rotting liver by fits of loud groaning vomiting" (1.108–110). It is, perhaps, no accident that the prominent appearance of his mother's ghost occurs again inside another temporary residence, the bordello, where the bed is the most necessary piece of furniture. Roman Catholicism and church-dominated Ireland itself are linked in Stephen's memory with the room of his dying mother: her final request—which Stephen denied—was for him to pray for her and, thus, reconvert to the faith. Stephen prefers to be out of doors partly because of these upsetting connotations that domesticity has for him. His most recent accommodation gives him one more impetus to prefer wandering under the open skies of Dublin: apart from the mental anguish, the place revolts him. The "kitchen"—a den in the martello tower—is shrouded in the thick smoke of burning. The "[s]tale, smoky air" (2.199) in Mr. Deasy's office at the Dalkey school disgusts him too. The headmaster's condescending and self-referential conversation, trite generalizations, and overt anti-Semitism aggravate Stephen's sense of discomfort. Anti-Semitism characterizes the mentality of people he rejects and who oppress him. Mr. Deasy's description of the Jews, ironically, applies to Stephen as well: "—They sinned against the light, . . . [a]nd you can see the darkness in their eyes. And that is why they are wanderers on the earth to this day" (2.361–63). Stephen, of course, also wanders about in the world homeless. He has nowhere to sleep on this day. Stephen could go to stay with the Gouldings, his "aunt Sara" and "uncle Richie." The thought crosses his mind on Sandymount strand, as the relatives reside on Strasburg Terrace nearby: "He halted. I have passed the way to aunt Sara's. Am I not going there? Seems not" (3.158–59). He yearns for fresh air, sunshine, and the breeze. "This wind is sweeter" (3.104), he says to himself; probably, he would find the atmosphere suffocating at the Gouldings. He does not intend to return to the Dedalus home, now in complete disarray since the mother's death. Simon Dedalus spends all his money in pubs; he even pawns the family furniture. Stephen knows about the misery of his sisters. He encounters Dilly Dedalus at the bookstalls where she has just bought herself a French primer for a penny. As one of the novel's most painful epiphanies unfolds, Stephen has a bad conscience, "[a]genbite of inwit" (10.879): he understands that his sisters have no hope of moving themselves out of their state of stagnation and misery. Dilly's pathetic attempt to learn French from a primer disconcerts him; however, with "healthy" egoism he knows that if he were to go back to them, they would pull him down too. Furthermore, for all his bad conscience, he does not offer a penny to his sisters; his salary is in his pocket, and later on, he will spend it freely and generously on drinks.

At the last station of his odyssey for the day, Stephen refuses to stay with the Blooms in Eccles Street. Bloom's day ends in his house where it also began. Unlike Stephen, who woke up on the middle level of a tower, Bloom steps out of bed on the ground floor on the morning of 16 June, and immediately hurries downstairs to the kitchen in the basement. Symbolically, Stephen tends to look up; his interests lie in a world of ideas and abstractions. Bloom, however, looks down at the world of objects. As they are together in Bloom's kitchen at night, Bloom examines the kettle and the pan on the stove, while Stephen looks up at the laundry line. The Latin words and mock-divine incantations signifying breakfast and the onset of Stephen's day yield their place to Bloom's conversation with the cat, the Eccles Street version of the "panther" in the martello tower. Bloom's breakfast kidney burns as the "three-egg fry-up" does in Mulligan's den; however, Bloom is not disgusted by the smell as Stephen is: he tucks in with relish.

Bloom likes his objects at home. He attaches the "utmost importance" to home life and suspects that Stephen's domestic experiences leave much to be desired (16.1177–79). Yet Bloom himself quite seriously entertains the idea of leaving Eccles Street for good. Besides his humiliating experiences in Dublin society, he cannot enjoy the desired state of the "family man" in a traditional, patriarchal setting. He shows Stephen his wife's photo, since a figure like the "ideal" Molly is what the young man lacks in his opinion: "a centre, even in the midst of the void." But, ironically, Bloom feels that he cannot avail himself of this center. A singer, Molly certainly differs from the stereotypical and traditional Dublin middle- or, rather, lower-middle-class housewife. She has a career, albeit a fairly inactive one. Nevertheless she has some professional acquaintances, such as Boylan, to whom Bloom has introduced her. On this day, Molly, for sure, "desanctifies" their bed, "the bed of conception and of birth, of consummation of marriage and of breach of marriage, of sleep and of death" (17.2119–21). The text does not provide sufficient information regarding the extent of Molly's adultery. Many Dublin men refer to her in more or less sexual terms, among them John Henry Menton, O'Madden Burke, and Simon Dedalus. Bloom suspects her of having betrayed him with no fewer than twenty-five men (17.2133–42), but his estimate seems highly unreasonable: Boylan may well be Molly's first lover. In the morning of 16 June 1904, Molly hides Boylan's letter under the pillow, and at night, as Bloom returns, he finds the physical reminders of Molly's encounter with Boylan in the bed: "What did his limbs, when gradually extended, encounter? New clean bed linen, additional odours, the presence of a human form, female, hers, the imprint of a human form, male, not his, some crumbs, some flakes of potted meat, recooked, which he removed" (17.2122–25). The disruption of customary objects disrupts Bloom's sense of physical stability. Apart from the signs of Boylan's presence earlier, which Molly has not bothered to clean away, the furniture has also been rearranged. He notices this after Stephen has left. The pieces have been moved and some of the books on the shelf are upside down.

Eventually, Bloom joins Molly in bed; the couple have not had full sexual intercourse for ten and a half years. Bloom remembers that in their home in Lombard Street West, before Rudy was conceived, they were contented. Then they started moving: they went to Raymond Terrace where Molly became pregnant with Rudy, then they moved to the City Arms Hotel before coming to

Eccles Street. Never since the birth and early death of the baby boy has their marriage been fully satisfactory. Molly confirms this in her monologue.

In Bely's *Petersburg* people dislike their homes, be they rich or poor. Some of them prefer the world of the streets whose many dangers still seem preferable to the dreadful visions and dreams inside the room. In *Ulysses*, Stephen gravitates away from enclosed areas. Bloom, however, feels secure inside buildings and feels less confident in the open: he is more vulnerable to gossip and hostility when outside the controllable environment of the room. Like Bely's Senator Ableukhov, Bloom enjoys the secure privacy of small enclosures: he seems particularly contented in the outhouse in the morning and, later on, in the bathtub in the public baths in Leinster Street. Wandering around without his keys contributes an additional element of insecurity to his day. No matter where Bloom and Stephen or the central figures in *Petersburg* are, a sense of dispossession surrounds them in the modern city.

In *Ulysses* no revolution is getting under way nor is anybody about to be murdered. Nevertheless, people turn to the street to avoid unpleasantness at home. Streets and squares, churches, museums, libraries, and pubs make up the public space in which to spend time. Strolling offers an opiate to Bloom for numbing unpleasant thoughts in "Lotus Eaters." He picks up a letter from Martha Clifford at the Westland Row post office. Her correspondence addresses him as Henry Flower and her own name may also be a pseudonym; they write amorous letters to each other even though they have never met. The "affair" with Martha excites Bloom mildly; he fleetingly remembers the letter waiting for him at the post office on his way to Tara Street. From the post office he goes to Sweny's, the chemist in Lincoln Place, before he enters the Leinster Street baths; he is too late to get back to Tara Street. During a meeting on Westland Row with M'Coy, Bloom fibs that his direction is "[n]owhere in particular" (5.85). He wants to get away from M'Coy to read Martha's letter undisturbed in Cumberland Street.

Bloom has chosen an unusual route from Eccles Street in North Dublin to the Westland Row post office on the southern side of the Liffey. He reaches Westland Row from Sir John Rogerson's Quay through Lime Street, crossing Townsend Street. The pattern of his path from the river to the post office forms the shape of a question mark (Hart and Knuth 1975, 25; McCarthy 1986, 24). Later, on his way to Barney Kiernan's from the Ormond Hotel, instead of walking up Arran Street from Ormond Quay Upper, he goes to the Four Courts, where he turns right into Greek Street and again right into Mary's Lane to get to the pub on the corner of Little Green Street (the continuation of Arran Street) and Little Britain Street. This time, his route resembles the shape of an upturned question mark (Nicholson 1988, 84). It seems that, at the very least, the pattern of his movements about the city allows him to objectify existential doubts he would not want to or could not verbalize. Bloom is looking for comforts in the city unavailable at his home: sex, in the forms of the slight thrill of Martha's letter and the more formidable thrill afforded by the voyeurism and masturbation on Sandymount beach; a nice hot bath; a hot lunch, as none awaits him at home. (It has been proposed that an indoor toilet and possibly even a bathroom are available in 7 Eccles Street [Nicholson 1988, 35], but it is a fact that Bloom uses neither.) For his meal, Bloom has to make do with a cold sandwich at Davy Byrne's; the Burton restaurant, which serves hot food, repulses him and the clientele does not appeal to him. He is a wily walker who, like Odysseus, tries to navigate safely about Dublin, avoiding unpleasantness. After leaving Davy Byrne's, Bloom changes course to avoid a "ravenous terrier" choking up its cud.

Dublin does not treat Bloom particularly well. Many of the people he meets throughout the day regard him with contempt. He is belittled several times: of all names it is his that happens to be misprinted as "L. Boom" in the newspaper column where the list of Dignam's mourners appears (16.1260). On the way to the cemetery he is the last person to get into the carriage and also the last one to alight. His attempts to establish contact with people often fail to elicit the expected response. On the way out of Glasnevin cemetery, Bloom addresses J. H. Menton, the solicitor, the former employer of the deceased man, to draw his attention to a dent in his hat:

—Excuse me sir, Mr Bloom said beside them.
They stopped.
—Your hat is a little crushed, Mr Bloom said pointing.
John Henry Menton stared at him for an instant without moving. . . .
—Thank you, he said shortly.
They walked on towards the gates.
Mr Bloom, chapfallen, drew behind a few paces so as not to overhear. . . .
Oyster eyes. Never mind. Be sorry after perhaps when it dawns on him.
Get the pull over him that way.
Thank you. How grand we are this morning. (6.1016–33)

Although he is a clever walker, he fails as a communicator. He knows that Menton is ill-disposed toward him, and it shows his naivety that he assumes that he can ingratiate himself by impolitely interrupting his conversation.

Bloom receives unfavorable treatment in his job too. His boss, Myles Crawford, is unfriendly to him in the newspaper office. Even the newsboys make fun of him: as he is walking down the street, they follow him, imitating his gait. Bloom feels that as soon as he turns his back on his companions, they start gossiping about him. In Barney Kiernan's pub, he makes the same mistake as with Menton in the cemetery: he wants to join a group of people—containing several Irish nationalists—who feel that he has no place among them, that he should not have come here in the first place. Moreover, he should not have left temporarily, allowing the gathered company to exchange vicious remarks about him in his absence. By the time he returns, he finds the atmosphere openly hostile and is nearly assaulted by the "citizen."

For all that, Bloom does not easily get despondent. Hunger rather than *Weltschmerz* produces his gloomy thoughts on transitoriness for a brief period. The scheme of planning a walk across Dublin without passing a pub is more in keeping with his generally cheerful disposition. On his daylong wandering, he looks for life's pleasurable aspects, out of harm's way, as, for instance, in the morning when he first leaves his house: "He crossed to the bright side, avoiding the loose cellarflap of number seventyfive" (4.77–78). Nevertheless, he is a disadvantaged walker: the mourning clothes on this particular day, his way of walking, and his looks make him conspicuous. For example, as Gerty MacDowell is looking at him on Sandymount beach, "[s]he could see at once by his dark eyes and his pale intellectual face that he was a foreigner..." (13.415–16). Being too noticeable, he cannot avoid M'Coy in Westland Row, who inadvertently reminds him of Molly's rather limited success as a singer and also of her infidelity. M'Coy's wife—another singer—has got a singing engagement, which reminds Bloom of Molly's proposed trip to Belfast where she is to sing at a concert in the Ulster Hall, organized by Boylan. Bloom is also noticed by Bantam Lyons. This meeting happens to be particularly unfortunate. Bantam Lyons scrutinizes Bloom's newspaper for information on horses running at a race later that day. He does not pay full attention to Bloom, who invites him to keep the paper that he was going to throw away (5.531–35). Clearly, Bloom never intended to refer favorably to the chances of a horse called "Throwaway," which will win the race, but his half-heard comment gives rise to anti-Semitic mutterings about Bloom's "unfair" access to moneymaking, even at the races.

When society treats Bloom unkindly, the elements favor him. On his way to the National Library, he suddenly catches sight of Boylan sauntering along Kildare Street and he manages to rush into the grounds of the National Museum to avoid an embarrassing meeting. Luckily for Bloom, the sun shines into Boylan's eyes, not his. The sun is behind Bloom as he is talking to Mrs. Breen in the street, allowing him to get her out of the way of a mentally unbalanced man: "Mr Bloom touched her funnybone gently, warning her. —Mind! Let this man pass. A bony form strode along the curbstone from the river, staring with a rapt gaze into the sunlight through a heavystringed glass. Tight as a skullpiece a tiny hat gripped his head. From his arm a folded dustcoat, a stick and an umbrella dangled at his stride. —Watch him, Mr Bloom said. He always walks outside the lampposts. Watch!" (8.293–99). When Bloom is making his getaway from the vicious "Citizen," he again, luckily for him, has his back to the sun. His opponent is blinded for a moment, like the Cyclops in *The Odyssey*. This saves Bloom from being hit by a biscuit tin hurled at him.

Notwithstanding his clever peripatetic tactics, Bloom feels happier and safer in well-enclosed nooks. He finds a relieving shelter in All Hallows Church, on the museum grounds in "Lestrygonians," and in the carriage to the cemetery. True enough, his companions embarrass him three times in the carriage: they do not let him finish his story; they discuss suicide, which, of course, is a painful topic for Bloom whose father took his own life; finally, the carriage passes Boylan. Yet, he feels safe and part of the group: in the carriage's enclosure, nobody can gossip about, or ally against, him. Bloom also feels comfortable in Davy Byrne's clean and friendly pub until they mention Boylan's name. In the evening, the engulfing darkness and the "seaweedy rocks" (13.348) offer him the privacy in which he can masturbate unnoticed.

Public respectability matters to Bloom greatly: while he certainly is not a person of means, he strives to maintain his independence and dignity. Whether he likes it or not, he is treated as, and feels like, something of an outsider; as a result, he can maintain a greater hermeneutic horizon from which to view his milieu than other Dubliners. Although as a walker of Dublin he shares many of these features with Stephen, Bloom comes closer to the figure of the flâneur. Stephen does not worry about whether he seems respectable to other walkers in the street. Besides, he is much less noticeable than Bloom: as he easily merges in with the crowd, he comes close to the type Walter Benjamin calls the badaud. His father does not see him as he passes in the funeral cortege; also, in "Aeolus" the two Dedaluses cross each other's paths without the son having to meet his father.

Stephen's acquaintances in the city treat him no better than his "friends" in the martello tower. In "Circe," Lynch mocks and abandons him and when he is beaten up, Kelleher fails to drive him home. The invisible walls of the city oppress him no less than they do Bloom. Stephen knows that unless he breaks away, his artistic talent will be destroyed. Unhappy walkers both, one coming from South Dublin, the other from the north of the city, Stephen and Bloom wander together for a short time before they separate, uncertain about their future direction.

Unlike in *Petersburg* and *Ulysses*, characters in *Berlin Alexanderplatz* must by necessity be good walkers: since they belong to the big city's "underworld," they need to know how best to turn the city to their advantage. In all three novels, characters benefit from the night that hides, even though it does not protect, them. In *Ulysses*, characters are neither criminals, as in Döblin's novel, nor frenzied victims of an ideologically and existentially supercharged environment, as in Bely's *Petersburg*. Their preference for night over day, however, suggests that they are similarly deprived, divided, and lonely twentieth-century urbanites, like their counterparts in the other novels. And yet, because of the fine weather, Dublin emerges with particular radiance on this day.

Joyce does not offer an overly positive picture of Dublin. He neglects the thriving theatrical life and the general fizz of the "Irish Renaissance." Mental paralysis, filth, drunkenness, and usurpation dominate the city of *Ulysses*; these impressions characterized the author's own experience. The urban lower-middle-class world appears with great sharpness, but the impoverished working class is absent from the novel's consciousness. Likewise, the smart Anglo-Irish upper class and the professional upper-middle classes are almost completely unrepresented here. Fashionable Stephen's Green and Merrion Square might as well not exist for Joyce's readers. (Merrion Square does appear in the text though: the lying-in hospital is on Holles Street, on the northeastern side of the square. However, the occupants of the area are of no interest whatsoever in the world of *Ulysses*.) The boys at Mr. Deasy's school, Armstrong, Cochrane, and Talbot, come from well-off Anglo-Irish, upper-middle-class families (Nicholson 1988, 9). We have a glimpse of Dublin's upper echelon merely in the parody of "Circe" when the "ladies" "punish" Bloom.

Joyce's landscape contains a world of people, their habits, institutions, and culture rather than descriptions of the physical environment. Parallel experiences among the novel's characters are predictable because of similarities between their social moorings (Herr 1986, 117). But, then, of course, the novel's three protagonists, Bloom, Molly, and Stephen, are also uncharacteristic Dubliners. Thanks to the polyphony of narrating voices and the effect of "parallax" no one character's opinions or observations dominate. Stephen looks at the sunlit bay in the morning and sees a bowl of green vomit (rather unflattering for the country whose symbolic color is green), but this does not remain the prevailing impression of the book. Various walkers follow in each other's footsteps and see the same shops and people, even the same clouds in the sky.

The novel's "message," if any, arises from a simultaneity of different perspectives on the same phenomena.

The inhabitants, the architecture, even the climate, have symbolic functions in Bely's *Petersburg*. They call to mind a mysterious center unique to the city. While Joyce's Dublin is not primarily a symbol, epiphanies clearly evoke a "larger picture." The model of the novel's composition is *pars pro toto* (Hart and Knuth 1975, 22) instead of Bely's "*totum pro parte.*" Like his creator, Bloom also shuns abstractions and mysticism and, instead, observes with sympathy the small things that make up the world around him, as the following passage illustrates: "By Brady's cottages a boy for the skins lolled, his bucket of offal linked, smoking a chewed fagbutt. A smaller girl with scars of eczema on her forehead eyed him, listlessly holding her battered caskhoop. Tell him if he smokes he won't grow. O let him! His life isn't such a bed of roses! Waiting outside pubs to bring da home. Come home to ma, da" (5.5–9). The collage of visual and mental images characterizes the milieu of poor Dubliners with a clearer focus than a more purely metaphoric-symbolic model, such as that in *Petersburg*, allows (Barta 1990, 311–12). Nevertheless, the last sentence of the passage above is epiphanic: it captures an insight into the core of truth signified in the details that Bloom sees. The juxtaposition of the naturalistic and the epiphanic leads to a transmaterial realm in the minds of textual characters and readers alike. In this dimension, boundaries between temporal and spatial categories, myth and fantasy, disintegrate. As Bloom is walking down the street in "Lestrygonians," the trams remind him of mutability, an ever-present, albeit not persistently depressing concern in *Ulysses*:

> Trams passed one another, ingoing, outgoing, clanging. Useless words. Things go on same, day after day: squads of police marching out, back: trams in, out.... Dignam carted off. Mina Purefoy swollen belly on a bed groaning to have a child tugged out of her. One born every second somewhere. Other dying every second.... Cityful passing away, other cityful coming, passing away too.... Houses, lines of houses, streets, miles of pavements, piledup bricks, stones.... Piled up in cities, worn away age after age. Pyramids in sand.... Slaves Chinese wall. Babylon. (8.476–90)

As has been suggested earlier, this passage must be seen in the context of Bloom's wanderings of the whole day: at this point, he is hungry and exhausted and, after attending Dignam's funeral, he is obviously distressed. The gloomy imagery of the passage does not burden the whole text. Bely's novel, however, is a heavily charged, apocalyptic piece of writing; it has been argued that Bely did not merely write about the apocalypse but, in fact, wrote his own version of this Biblical event (Bethea 1989, 130). Whereas Bloom momentarily contemplates the futility of human endeavors, Nikolai Apollonovich opts to change his way of life completely: he goes to Egypt—the symbolical realm of death—before converting to the mystical teachings of the Ukrainian philosopher, Skovoroda, and leading a life away from the city. In the overtly apocalyptic symbolism of *Petersburg*, the narrator awaits destruction to come from the East. The only apocalyptic gesture in *Ulysses* occurs in "Circe" when Stephen smashes the lamp with his ashplant: "He lifts his ashplant high with both hands and smashes the chandelier. Time's livid final flame leaps and, in the following darkness, ruin of all space, shattered glass and toppling masonry" (15.4242–45). The act is facetious, since the only destruction that results is that the light goes out in the room and sixpence worth of damage is done to the lamp shade.

The mysterious realm appears in *Ulysses* gradually. While Buck Mulligan's own personality hides disguised, he seems to understand the interrelatedness of some phenomena to an unusual extent. He succeeds in tormenting Stephen by delving into his most private concerns. He instantly notices Bloom's interest in Stephen and attributes it to Bloom's supposedly homosexual proclivities: "—The wandering jew, Buck Mulligan whispered with clown's awe. Did you see his eye? He looked upon you to lust after you" (9.1209–10). While Mulligan only vaguely intimates an ability to draw on supernatural intelligence, in M'Intosh Joyce presents a figure of considerably greater uncertainty. Some critics have identified M'Intosh with Joyce. Thomas suggests that Joyce returns to Dublin as a ghost. He quotes Frank Budgen, who claimed to have seen Joyce in a brown mackintosh in Zurich when he was writing *Ulysses* (1982, 70). According to Marilyn French, Bloom's meditation at night concerning M'Intosh's identity is really asking who wrote the book and where the author stands (1976, 236). M'Intosh seems to appear out of nowhere at the funeral, and he disappears equally mysteriously. Nobody seems to know him. His "name" arises from a misunderstanding: "—And tell us, Hynes said, do you know that fellow in the, fellow was over there in the.... He looked around. —Macintosh. Yes, I saw him, Mr Bloom said. Where is he now? —M'Intosh, Hynes said scribbling, I don't know who he is" (6.891–95). The man in the mackintosh appears several more times, but the text does not clarify the mystery surrounding him. He crosses the road outside the Holles Street hospital as the viceroy's cavalcade approaches; at Burke's pub in "Oxen in the Sun" we learn that he is known as "Bartle the Bread." Bloom's dead grandfather, Virág, makes his ghostly appearance also wearing a brown mackintosh; and in "Circe" a man comes downstairs in the bordello and puts on a mackintosh and a hat. Zoe refers to him as the devil (15.2696). M'Intosh's opaque presence in the novel suggests the existence of the unpredictable and unknowable aspects of life in the modern city; like the White Domino in *Petersburg*, M'Intosh symbolizes confusion rather than any specific quality or entity. As Robert Crosman suggests, he is "[n]umber thirteen at the funeral, he is Christ or Judas. Wandering through Dublin, he is Odysseus or the Wandering Jew. Popping up from graveyards and trapdoors he is Satan . . . or Christ resurrected" (1968, 135).

For the novel's characters and readers alike, history and myth occupy a special realm. The narrators and narrating characters who share the contents of their consciousness with the reader are not aware of the Homeric structure. If the narrative offers one anchor in the novel's "parallax," surely the other is the classical epic of Odysseus of which the reader is conscious. A "fourth dimension" possesses great signifying power in Bely's *Petersburg*: ambassadors of that realm penetrate the city and appear to determine the fates of its inhabitants. The power of Shishnarfne or the Turanian lies in an entirely spiritual/mythical, rather than historical, past. Joyce is much more skeptical: transmaterial figures in *Ulysses* tend to be weak and transparent. Stephen repeats his "Non Serviam" to his mother's ghost (15.4229), which haunts him and attempts to force him back to Irish conventions and Christianity. He also rejects "Old Gummy Granny," "poor old Ireland," who intends to remind him of his supposedly patriotic duty (15.4587–88). And when the Virág ancestors—Bloom's father and grandfather—appear in "Circe," they neither frighten anyone nor are they imbued with any great symbolical value. Nevertheless, the thought of death and the dead clearly preoccupies Joyce's characters. The cityscape, as in *Petersburg*, contains "transitory" regions: the proximity of water invites thoughts of suicide, offering the space of transition from time to timelessness. Nikolai Apollonovich thinks of suicide on a bridge and so do Stephen and Bloom (8.52). As the men catch sight of Reuben J. Dodd in Bloom's carriage en route to the cemetery, a story is told about how Dodd's son was saved when he jumped into the Liffey attempting to drown himself. Stephen—who is terrified of water—ponders upon death in water several times during the day.[4] In "Proteus" he contemplates drowning: "Five fathoms out there. Full fathom five thy father lies. At one, he said. Found drowned. . . . A corpse rising saltwhite from the undertow. . . . There he is. Hook it quick. Pull. Sunk though he be beneath the watery floor. We have him. Easy now" (3.470–74). Water reminds him of his own sinful conception: "Wombed in sin darkness I was too, made not begotten. By them, the man with my voice and my eyes and a ghostwoman with ashes on her breath" (3.45–47). To Nikolai Apollonovich, standing on the bridge in *Petersburg*, the thought of suicide in water and the fluids of conception, in addition to the feeling of disgust regarding his parents' sexuality, also appear simultaneously. The idea of drowning in *Ulysses* extends metaphorically to characterize life in Ireland in general. Stephen fears that if he develops closer ties with his family, and with their Irish "paralysis," he will "drown" with them (10.876). Water also reminds him of the bile vomited up by his dying mother.

Water, particularly the idea of the Dead Sea, reminds Bloom of metempsychosis and makes him wonder about the possibility of a new life with Martha. Water and metempsychosis are logically associated: Bloom is sitting in the lying-in hospital while Mina Purefoy is being delivered of a baby. Birth, like death, means a transition from the "otherworldly" into three-dimensional space. Bridges lead from the known to the unknown in Bely's novel, and the function of doors is similar. The phenomenology of doors preoccupies Bloom too. He wonders about the *mezuzah*, whose name he cannot recall, that his Jewish grandfather had fixed to the door-frame: "That brought us out of the land of Egypt and into the house of bondage. Something in all those superstitions because when you go out never know what dangers" (13.1158–60). He feels safe only when in control both of the "door of egress" and the "door of ingress." The thought of not having his keys on him preoccupies him all day, not least because of the imaginary and real dangers that await him at home and in the city. Stephen, who has no physical or spiritual home in Ireland, does not possess keys either. At night, as they part in Bloom's garden, Stephen sets off into the dark and the unknown. Bloom retraces his steps to the "house of bondage" (17.1022); he feels that his house does not really offer him a great deal more stability than the biblical Egypt did to the people of Israel. Although he asks Molly "to get his breakfast in bed with a couple of eggs" (which is an unusual act of self-assertion in their household), nothing at all seems to indicate that 17 June will be any different from the previous day.

In spite of the thousands of incidents that comprise the plot of *Ulysses*, very little has changed in the lives of the characters by the end of the novel. In *Petersburg*, on the other hand, the world—as the main characters know it— effectively disappears. Instead of the trivia and tiny details that dominate the surface of reality in *Ulysses*, Bely imposes a hierarchy of values in his attempt to recreate classical mythopoeia. While irrational forces and apocalyptic expectations prevail in Bely's "exactly inexact" Petersburg, "scatology" is at least of as much, if not greater, interest to Joyce as eschatology (Cornwell 1989, 46). Authorial consciousness places characters under constant surveillance in *Petersburg*. The mythical extends a sense of timelessness in whose service and under whose control history stands. Thus, everything is linked with everything else. In *Ulysses*, however, the supernatural, the world of the dead, the mythical, and the historical invite a variety of interpretations; no authority figure in the text has imposed a "correct" one. Joyce's sweeping parody debunks his "fourth dimension." Bely's irony and his use of the grotesque do not, of course, extend to parodying the "center" from which "cerebral play" is regulated. *Ulysses* ends without closure because history, time, and space are perceived as relative in an Einsteinian "jocoserious" (17.369) universe where a "very short space of time" is measured "through very short times of space" (3.11–12).

In Joyce's plural text, signifiers liberate themselves from a monolithic meaning. This lessens the authority of "History" and "Myth." Irish and English history and legend, the Hebrew Old Testament, and the Christian New Testament, in addition to the world of classical mythology, intermingle with the real and pseudoreal world of Joyce's Dublin on 16 June 1904. Bloom receives a "throwaway" from a "sombre Y.M.C.A. young man." The leaflet announces the coming of "Elijah" and that a Dr. John Alexander Dowie, an American "restorer of the church of Zion," will be commenting upon the event. Bloom throws "Elijah"—the handbill—into the river. As textual signifiers, both "Elijah" and "throwaway" have several meanings and keep recurring in the text. In "Cyclops," both "Elijah" from the "throwaway"—the leaflet, that is—and Throwaway the horse—which wins the Gold Cup race—establish analogies with Bloom. As was discussed earlier, because of a misunderstanding, Bloom as a Jew is attributed psychic powers giving him foreknowledge of winning horses, among all other supposed advantages. The anti-Semitic discussion takes place during his temporary absence from the company in Barney Kiernan's pub. As they receive the returning Bloom with drunken fury, Bloom defends himself using powerful arguments against the "citizen's" rhetoric of hatred. He is like Elijah, the ninth-century B.C.E. Hebrew prophet, who proclaimed his God's vengeance with great force. The ending of "Cyclops" offers one of the best illustrations in the book of how the lofty and the commonplace, myth and daily life, complement each other rather than forming any kind of hierarchy: "And there came a voice out of heaven, calling: *Elijah! Elijah!* And He answered with a main cry: *Abba! Adonai!* And they beheld Him even Him, ben Bloom Elijah, amid clouds of angels ascend to the glory of the brightness at an angle of fortyfive degrees over Donohoe's in Little Green street like a shot off a shovel" (12.1914–18; italics in the original).

Thanks to the recurrence of the same motifs, various parts of the text establish a richly dialogic relationship with each other even when no clear thematic relationship exists. Before going to Barney Kiernan's pub, Bloom "comments" on nationalist aspirations: at the end of the "Sirens" chapter, as he reads in a shop window the "last words" of the Irish patriot, Robert Emmet, he loudly breaks wind, taking advantage of the noise of a passing tram:[5]

Seabloom, greaseabloom viewed last words. Softly.
When my country takes her place among.
Prrprr.
Must be the bur.
Fff! Oo. Rrpr.
Nations of the earth. No-one behind. She's passed. *Then and not till then.*
Tram kran kran kran. Good oppor. Coming. Krandlkrankran. I'm sure it's the burgund. Yes. One, two. *Let my epigraph be.* Kraaaaaa. *Written. I have.*
Pprrpffrrppfff.
Done. (11.1284-94—italics in original)

In the next chapter, the blindly nationalistic "Citizen's" "response" with its intolerant and singleminded tone matches Bloom's "eloquence."

The technique of juxtaposing often prevents historical themes from obtaining a rhetorically privileged position: the name of the ancient Irish king, Brian Boru, enters the text as "Brian Boroimhe house"—a pub—which the funeral cortege passes north of the Royal Canal.[6] Thomas Moore's statue is well placed over a street urinal, according to Bloom, in light of Moore's song, "The Meeting of the Waters" (Lehan 1988, 252). Bloom, too, has witnessed "history": once he picked up Charles Stewart Parnell's hat as the latter was engaged in a struggle. Parnell's brother, a tangential character in *Ulysses*, bears great resemblance to the late politician, but he is a drab and insignificant figure who prefers a game of chess to attending the meeting of the City Council.

Among the many voices of the present and the past, the most polytropic character in Joyce's Dublin is language itself. Recurring motifs with multiple signifieds operate in all contexts. As the keyless couple, Stephen and Bloom, wander about, "keys" become endowed with symbolical meaning. As Stephen sits drunk and dejected in Bella Cohen's bordello, he touches the keys of the piano whilst contemplating his sorry, homeless condition; he lacks the keys to open any door he can call his own. Also in "Circe," Bloom remembers his father, Rudolph, reprimanding him for the bad company he kept and for leaving "the house of his father . . . and the god of his fathers Abraham and Jacob" (15.261-62). Listening to his father, Bloom is standing *"wearing gent's sterling silver waterbury keyless watch"* (15.270; italics in the original). Besides its primary meaning, keylessness within the text connects with the concept of rootlessness: Bloom has lost the key to the symbolical house of his fathers. His unaccomplished business of the day also has to do with "keys": he is designing an advertisement for Mr. Alexander Keyes, "tea, wine and spirit merchant" (7.143). Keys symbolize one of the central issues in the novel, homelessness and dispossession. No wonder that Bloom associates keys with home rule: " — The idea, Mr Bloom said, is the house of keys. You know, councillor, the Manx parliament. Innuendo of home rule" (7.149–50; Senn 1972).

It is not my purpose in this study to address the elaborate system of textual references in *Ulysses*. It will suffice to list some peripatetic leitmotifs that circulate, and interrelate with each other, within the novel's discourse. The sun helps Bloom all day, blinding his adversaries, preventing them from seeing him. The sun's rays also remind him of his daughter, Milly: "Quick warm sunlight came running from Berkeley Road, swiftly, in slim sandals, along the brightening footpath. Runs, she runs to meet me, a girl with gold hair on the wind" (4.240–43). "Sun" as the homophone of "son" also reminds Bloom of his dead child, Rudy. To Bloom's mind, the boy's death accounts for his domestic unhappiness. He dreams of domestic bliss in a sunlit, Mediterranean place. Sunshine and warmth are necessary for the life of flowers; Bloom's pseudonym in his correspondence with Martha Clifford is Henry Flower. The German version of Henry, Heinrich, originally means "home ruler" and flower in Hungarian is *virág*. The Virágs, Bloom's ancestors, came from their original home in the city of Szombathely in Hungary.

In an advertisement, which is on Bloom's mind, home is connected to "Plumtree's Potted Meat." He is reminded of the product as he walks about town all day. Ironically he finds bits of Plumtree's potted meat in his bed at night, alongside other reminders of Boylan's presence there earlier. "Plums" signify frustration and dispossession for Stephen: hence the "Parable of the Plums" that was discussed earlier.

The concerted voices of the text prevail over the force of any one individual voice. Evgeny Zamyatin suggested in his article, "Andrei Bely," that the languages in *Ulysses* and *Petersburg* are Joyce's and Bely's, respectively, and not English and Russian (Zamyatin 1970, 243). Lack of a central narrative voice in *Ulysses* places even greater emphasis than in *Petersburg* on the chorus of interior monologues, streams of consciousness, complete or fragmentary conversation and remarks made by narrating voices. In *Ulysses*, as in the other two novels, the peripatetic characters identify with the city, which, however, does not identify with its walkers. The protagonist of *Stephen Hero* searches for "epiphanies" in the streets of Dublin to illuminate the city's meaning. Bloom suspects "swindle" behind the city's mystery, suggesting that a center of intelligence might exist but lies beyond the citizens' reach (8.488). Names fail to establish true identity, as "M'Intosh," "L. Boom," "Henry Flower" or "Ulysses" aptly demonstrate. The individual is unable to comprehend his own "essence," let alone his city's. We can only speculate about the missing subject complement in the incomplete sentence Bloom writes in the sand: "I. . . . AM. A" (13.1258–64).

It has repeatedly been argued that *Ulysses* was a book that could not be read, only reread. The last letter "s" of *Ulysses* in Molly's final "Yes" curves back to "s" in "Stately," the first word of the novel. Creative readers have, by the end of the novel, come to understand much more than any of the characters and are well prepared to reorganize the information the text supplies and carve out new paths in the maze. The novel is not finished on the last page, only the waking day of the characters is. Stephen and Bloom will wander again on the next day, which will dawn some time in the infinite future, as long as there are readers whose imagination will call them forth from the printed page.

CHAPTER 4

Walking in the Shadow of Death
Berlin Alexanderplatz

Ever since its publication in October 1929, Döblin's *Berlin Alexanderplatz* has been compared to *Ulysses*.[1] Döblin read Joyce's novel with great enthusiasm and he reviewed it very favorably. He considered *Ulysses* a useful source of stylistic devices. With regard to his own novel, he even admitted that it was "good wind" in his sails (Bance 1982, 59). Numerous studies have examined how and to what degree Joyce influenced Döblin in the writing of his novel (Komar 1981, 334; Mitchell 1971). To point out where and how Döblin changed his own manuscript in order to imitate Joyce is of little comparative interest, since all authors, consciously or unconsciously, write against an intertextual horizon. As Roland Barthes says, an author's "only power is to mix writings, to counter the ones with the others in such a way as never to rest on any one of them" (Barthes 1977, 146). Döblin very eloquently defends his works against charges of "plagiarism" in the unpublished typescript of a lecture: "Joyce is a magnificent writer, a pioneer of style, and thus also of narrative technique. I myself am not able to analyze whether and which Joycean influences are demonstrable in my last book. I do know, however, that Joyce has nothing to do with the essential parts of my work; only peripheral similarities are concerned" (quoted from Mitchell 1976, 149). Andrei Bely, writing in a different cultural context, is safe from being accused of copying a contemporary author in creating a protagonist out of his city. His novel preceded *Ulysses* by six years and *Berlin Alexanderplatz* by thirteen.

The claim of some critics that *Berlin Alexanderplatz* is the first and most successful evocation of modern Berlin in German literature is by no means exaggerated (Dollenmayer 1988, 3; Ziolkowski 1969, 107). Like *Ulysses* or *Petersburg*, it had a significant impact on the style of fiction in the language of its origin (Durzak 1979, 186). Unlike the other two novels, which have, up to this day, attracted mainly students and scholars of literature, *Berlin Alexanderplatz* enjoyed considerable popular success when it appeared, and very soon after its publication, the first film version was released. Döblin's novel was well received by all groups of the reading public. His publisher, Samuel Fischer, clearly eager to market the new novel as a bestseller, urged Döblin to add the subtitle "The Story of Franz Biberkopf" to the original title, *Berlin Alexanderplatz*. Even the most conventional readers seemed to express interest in Döblin's novel: a concerned German "Bürger" warned the publisher that the novel's insights into German life were unflattering, and the book, therefore, should not be publicized abroad (Durrani 1987, 142). Apart from serving as a splendid illustration of German bourgeois nationalist "cosmopolitanism," such a statement also reveals that the "average" reader, whom neither *Petersburg* nor *Ulysses* ever attracted, regarded the novel as a mimetically accurate representation of aspects of Berlin life in the late 1920s. While the city is largely symbolical in *Petersburg*, in Döblin's novel it stands for a most concrete place. The city in *Ulysses* is similarly "real," but the main characters who roam the streets are deemed as outsiders and they differ from "typical" Dubliners. *Berlin Alexanderplatz* is peopled by types most contemporary readers would immediately recognize. The Berlin public of 1929 was much more familiar with the world depicted in the novel than many of the early readers of *Ulysses* and *Petersburg* were with the milieu captured in these works. Döblin's Berlin is lacking in aristocratic or middle-class heroes: we see mainly the city of the lower classes, of prostitutes, pimps, and criminals. This is the world of the streets that knows no glitter or elegance, but it throbs with the rhythms of modern life, evoked by cars, trams, and unceasing construction work. This scenery prompted Walter Muschg to define the novel as "the ripest fruit of Berlin Futurism" (1961, 221).

The novel is not entitled simply "Berlin." Unlike other European capital cities, Berlin is essentially an amalgamation of several autonomous administrative units and each has a different character. Alexanderplatz is an independent part, with unique features of its own, named after the central square in the eastern part of the city. Like Joyce, who had an unusually thorough knowledge of the Irish capital, Döblin too was intimately familiar with this particular area of Berlin. His characters do not roam Kurfürstendamm, Tiergarten, or Unter den Linden. They live, and walk about, in the vicinity of a proletarian square with a historical name that nobody in the novel troubles to identify; it was named in honor of the visit of Russia's Tsar Alexander in 1805. Between the end of World War I and 1933, when he emigrated from Germany, Döblin practiced neurology from his office at Halleschen Tor, which was within walking distance of Alexanderplatz. He also did an internship in the Buch asylum in 1906 and 1907, and he published a description of a case of hysteria similar to Franz Biberkopf's. But even many years before he became a physician in East-Central Berlin, Döblin had already been exposed to the environment and mood that inform his novel: he came from a working-class Berlin family himself.

The focus of the novel is the present. While the characters walk about the city in *Ulysses* or *Petersburg*, in their minds they simultaneously explore the past of their family and culture. The descent through the consciousness in these novels is just as important as the physical walk that shapes the plot. In *Berlin Alexanderplatz*, however, neither the city nor the characters seem to have a past; the old buildings are being demolished, the streets are lined with newer and bigger houses, and beneath the surface runs the newly constructed underground train system. The past of Döblin's characters is irrelevant, and human life is compressed into a few biographical facts. The background of the most important characters, Franz and Reinhold, is almost completely shrouded in obscurity. In the montage episodes dozens of characters appear; most of them do not know any of the novel's central characters. In these side-stories, the narrating voice surveys entire human lives grotesquely abbreviated into a few short sentences (Dollenmayer 1988, 95). The notion of novelty, the process of never-ending construction work, and the lack of a sense of the past reveal a thematic analogy between *Berlin Alexanderplatz* and the contemporary American city novel which is best represented by Dos Passos' *Manhattan Transfer* (1925). Surely, Döblin was aware of *Manhattan Transfer*, whose German translation, like that of *Ulysses*, came out in 1927.

In his novel, Döblin follows a similar pattern to that of Bely and Joyce. The perspective of walking manages to create fiction out of the throbbing experience of urban modernity in *Berlin Alexanderplatz* as well. Here, again, it is of primary interest how the storytelling voices come to terms with the city, against which the fate of Franz Biberkopf is set. Above all, it is his story that is being told in the novel. In order to see what sort of lived-in, human space Biberkopf's Berlin is, we must follow him, the Berlin walker, and see how he relates to those around him, and how people move about in their city.

For Joyce, fewer than twenty-four hours suffice to evoke Dublin; he is not interested in the alteration of the course of human life in the city, and shies away from straightforward solutions to the problems, which he illuminates rather than resolves. His doubts about the validity of any ideology distinguish him from Bely, for whom life in St. Petersburg is determined by a spiritual realm. Bely's primary interest is not in the influence of the city on its people: the contradictory forces that are responsible for their existence unite Petersburg and its inhabitants. As we saw earlier, the duration of the plot is only a few days, not including the epilogue, which, together with the last paragraph of the final chapter in the novel, foreshadows the fate of the Ableukhov family. Time is as concentrated as the cramped habitats of the population.

By contrast, the elaborate epic plot in *Berlin Alexanderplatz* takes from the autumn of 1927 to the beginning of 1929 to evolve. *Berlin Alexanderplatz* resembles *Ulysses* in containing an extensive number of narrating voices, which vary considerably in their stylistic and ideological charges. As is the case in *Petersburg* and *Ulysses*, Döblin's many-voiced narrative creates the novel's image of Berlin. Döblin consciously attempted to remove his own direct authorial voice from the novel. In his *Aufsätze zur Literatur* (*Essays on Literature*) he defines his understanding of omniscience as follows: "I am not I but the streets, the streetlamps, various events, and nothing beyond that" (Ryan 1981, 421; my translation).

Unlike in Bely and Joyce, Döblin's narrative about Franz Biberkopf, a lower-class Berlin Everyman, projects a sense of "social responsibility." We learn how Franz's life, after suffering three blows by fate, "acquires a meaning": "To listen to this, and to meditate on it, will be of benefit to many who, like Franz Biberkopf, live in a human skin, and, like this Franz Biberkopf, ask more of life than a piece of bread and butter" (2), the narrator comments in the prologue. Again, unlike *Ulysses* or *Petersburg*, Döblin's novel has one central protagonist, besides the figure of the city, of course. Nevertheless, in his ordinariness, Franz Biberkopf comes across as less of an individual and more as a representative of a social milieu. Stephen Dedalus and Bloom, or Bely's Ableukhovs, occupy a higher social standing and are better informed about the world than Franz. As a result, they have greater mobility and are less tied to their immediate environment: the Ableukhov family leaves Petersburg, and Stephen and Bloom consider leaving Dublin. For Franz, however, no alternative to being in the Alexanderplatz district is available other than prison or hospital (Scherpe 1989, 167).

In chapter 1.2, without any comment, the narrator simply presents the coat of arms of the city of Berlin together with the emblems of all the major municipal departments that ensure its administration: "Trade and Commerce, Street Cleaning and Transport, Health Department, Underground Construction, Art and Culture, Traffic, Municipal Savings Bank, Gas Works, Fire Department, Finance and Tax Office." In this careful inventory, one department is conspicuous by its absence: the police. This silence characterizes the ironical narrating voice that is very powerful in the novel. Omitting the police seems "tactful" inasmuch as the narrative recounts the "careers" of burglars, pimps, and prostitutes.

It is this storyteller who offers facetious prefaces before chapters and whose irony resounds in numerous section headings. Thanks to these epic summaries, he is in a position to create certain expectations for the reader. He implies a conventional reading public, bred in the cliched concepts of bourgeois "decency" and "morality." The reader, whom the prologue leads to expect a *Bildungsroman*, soon finds him/herself surrounded by marionettes instead of characters of the classic realist tradition. No doubt, such headings as "Reinhold's Black Wednesday but this chapter may be skipped" are designed to puzzle the implied reader and disappoint his or her logical expectations. The pseudo-scientific statements about social law or sexual behavior also tend to shock such a reader's complacency; these insertions refer to Franz's conduct and create a dehumanizing effect. The precise scientific description of the physical laws responsible for the violent death of Franz's girlfriend, Ida, grotesquely distorts the moral implications of Franz's violence against her. Clearly, the greatest challenge for the implied reader lies in the fact that not only does the plot not belong to a *Bildungsroman* but also it is located in a modernist rather than a representational text. The city is impossible to grasp for walker and narrator alike: instead of a narrative about the city, the city itself narrates (Scherpe 1989, 167–68). The ironical storytelling persona plays with the stuff of reality; he keeps commenting on what he sees in the future. In half a page we learn the entire course of a boy's life to come; his only connection to the main plot is that he happens to live in the same part of Berlin at the same time as Franz. He is called Max Rust and we see him board a number four train at the Lothringerstrasse stop. The details of his future life are grotesquely reduced in the manner of newspaper headlines (Dollenmayer 1988, 73). Here, again, the implied reader may very well feel frustrated as Döblin's text mocks the omniscient narrative mode of representational, positivist realism. Döblin makes the point that however privy we may be to all the data, we still do not understand whatever transpires behind the facts.

Without any comment, the narrative accommodates various sorts of linguistic debris from the street: the routes of tram lines, as displayed in the stop, the weather forecast, and items of interest read in the paper, heard on the radio, or gathered from street gossip. These present a very broad, almost universal, background from which to observe Franz Biberkopf's story. The network of montage vastly expands the range of experience that founds the conventional single-, double-, or even triple-decker realist novel. However, Döblin "decomposes" this Berlin reality that the narrative captures (Elm 1991, 130). For example, advertisements are inserted into the text; their original pragmatic function is to persuade potential buyers to purchase. In this attempt, they portend a false promise of security, order, and stability, which they attribute to the products for sale. As the narrating persona twists the original function of the discourse of consumerism, it performs a highly self-conscious act; after all, the storytelling voice in the novel at large also leads the implied reader to false expectations. At one point, commercial arguments promoting bananas are incorporated. Accordingly, bananas are the cleanest fruit and thus safest for children because their skin keeps insects out. But the narrator turns the issue around by adding that bananas are not safe from such insects and bacilli as are capable of penetrating the skin. The image of the outer skin protecting, or not protecting, whatever is inside contains a broad metaphor about the well-being of the citizen in a city. Similar ideas of an outside threat penetrating the walls of security (the banana's, the home's, the city's) occupy an important symbolic role in *Petersburg* and are also central to the consciousness of *Ulysses*.

It is through the montage of details of the animate and inanimate world of the city, and through the diverse narratorial voices, that a strong plot is developed, based on Franz's story and spiced with the pseudointention of "edifying" the implied reader. One of the story-telling personae is the "monteur-narrator." He resembles the author constructing the juxtaposition of the various narrators, which, in itself, creates a montage. The chorus of narrating voices reenacts some of the aural impressions to which the walker is exposed. The boxing commentator's style of the prologue and the street-ballad tone of the summaries introducing each book are full of the sounds of working-class Berlin. The text's montage is comprised of dozens of side episodes; they stand as isolated instances, but the similarities of each with the others and with the fate of Franz Biberkopf endow certain recurring themes (for example, how naive credulity and lack of compassion ultimately result in loss) with leitmotivic force. The episodes are narrated sketchily in a journalistic manner rather than in fully developed subplots. In passages where the Berlin montage dominates, Franz's story is temporarily obscured. Most of the fragments recount the failures of people like Franz, however. As a result, the dedramatized montage segments support Franz's line in the plot (Furthman-Durden 1986, 449; Scherpe 1989, 169; Dollenmayer 1988, 68).

Döblin's novel is a storehouse of modernist techniques (the viewpoint constantly shifts, the narrative is a compendium of montage effects, and of allusions to dozens of texts), yet the way of representing Berlin is mimetic. This is not the case either in *Ulysses* or *Petersburg*. Bely's city, in every corpuscle, is connected to the cognitive system of symbols that underpins the creative intelligence of the writer. In *Ulysses*, Dublin offers the starting points for meditations that reach into the inner realms of human consciousness. Döblin, however, reproduces the phenomena of the city with a sharp sense of modernist sensitivity. The parts of the plot that explicitly focus on Franz Biberkopf deal with his movements from his room to the streets, and his wanderings in the city. His explicit purpose is that he wants to start an "honest" life; his walking, thus, has special significance in that he is a "seeker." After his release from Tegel prison, he tries to establish a lower-middle-class existence in the Alexanderplatz district. His attempt to lead a decent life is futile, however: without any initial funds and contacts and, importantly, an education, such a status is unattainable. As opposed to the walkers of *Petersburg* or *Ulysses*, Franz has no definite abode: he moves from place to place, his addresses change even between episodes. The novel's title itself, which refers to a central transport stop where several major tram and railway lines intersect, conveys the sense of constantly being on the go (Lewis 1976, 105). Franz belongs to nobody: he has no wife, children, parents, or other relatives. His girlfriends and acquaintances keep changing like his rented rooms. He is unable to settle down; his failure to establish stable relationships based on mutual trust is largely responsible for this. Franz expects the women who love him to work for him as prostitutes. He is a "picaresque" hero in that he is never at home anywhere; the narrative also emphasizes this point in accounting for some of the "sensational" aspects of his progress in the manner of "Moritat" storytelling. Indeed, Franz does not fit categories easily: he is not a law-abiding citizen, but then he is not a real criminal either; he is not a shirker, but nor is he properly employed, except in the novel's sketchily outlined conclusion. Franz's sexuality is also ambiguous. He has heterosexual relations, but he appears to be more strongly drawn to Reinhold than to his "girls." Swapping each other's women certainly indicates the possibility of their repressed homoerotic desire. Reinhold's homosexuality is confirmed when he is in prison and falls in love with his fellow prisoner. Franz is not imprisoned during the course of much of the novel, but he always faces the possibility of being arrested. Socially, he stands between the lumpen-proletariat and the lower-middle class. Politically, he is seeking "order," which complements "decency," and he flirts with both the Communists and the Nazis (Scherpe 1989, 174; Mahlendorf 1986, 96).

Franz's circle is comprised of unemployed people who make a living out of illegal activities. His friends are thieves and burglars. The only significant, recurring element in the novel that connects the present with the past is the memory of Franz's murder of his "girl," Ida. For this he was sentenced to serve four years in Berlin's Tegel prison. After his release, he did not have any place to go except his former environment, the sordid Alexanderplatz area. This is his Berlin where he feels at home. In the unfavorable economic climate of the late twenties, the only jobs he, as an unskilled person ("an erstwhile cement- and transport-worker"), can get are temporary: he works as a news-vendor, a barker, and also deals in haberdashery. Thus, even when he is employed, which is rarely, Franz has no choice but to be in the streets. His enterprises, which are all connected with the "open spaces" of the city—streets, squares, beerhalls, and cafes—end badly for him: he becomes jobless, he loses his arm, and he loses all his lovers, even Mieze, for whom he truly cares.

The experiences of Franz Biberkopf echo those of his fellow-Berliners in Alexanderplatz. Throughout the novel, the "monteur" narrator keeps the streets under his surveillance. In significant sections he forgets about everything except what he sees; he scans the passers-by and looks into unrelated people's flats. Apparently, he is aware only of the details he is reporting. The organizing consciousness is the author's, but it is the narrator who provides the vivisection of Alexanderplatz by the use of the montage. As he keeps roaming the Alexanderplatz area, he observes people's lives; in fact, Franz himself could easily have read, or heard, about some of the events. Readers are clearly better informed than any narrator or character: they can survey the spectrum of all the gloomy episodes, including Franz's story of dispossession. Futile as their lives may be, the people in the streets of Joyce's Dublin do not feel tense at all times, even if they are "outsiders" like Bloom and Stephen. Walkers in *Petersburg* move about nervously; the city around them is like an explosive device but it is moored in its historical and mythical past. In Berlin nothing is permanent; the city is like some giant who needs all the energy he can obtain in order to demolish and build.

The aesthetic representation of impermanence calls for the use of montage. This is certainly the most appropriate form allowing Döblin to convey his experience of Berlin; in fact, no better aesthetic device exists to capture the violence and changeability of the modern metropolis. Bely experiments with the technique of the collage, and Joyce uses it quite extensively (Barta 1990, 214). In Döblin's case, because of the novel's close analogy with the techniques of film, montage seems a more appropriate term to use than collage. In his review of *Ulysses*, Döblin talked about the impact on the novel both of the newspaper and of film (Dollenmayer 1988, 65–68). Walter Ruttman's 1927 documentary, *Berlin. The Symphony of a Great City*, used the technique of montage and, no doubt, proved an influential source for *Berlin Alexanderplatz*. Collage creates a stronger aural effect whilst montage conveys the visual experience more sharply: both can aptly capture the loneliness of the individual surrounded by the lively city. In one of the novel's episodes, a couple lose their child because the doctor is not available to help; another couple commit suicide: "Alex and Vera had planned to get married, but economic conditions did not permit their conjugal union" (253). Others, like the criminals Beese and Bornemann, try to hide in Berlin, but get caught. Franz and Mieze stand out, of course, because their stories are fully developed. But when Mieze's storyline draws to a close upon her violent death, she joins the canvas of Berliners whose fates resemble her own. It is only at this point that we are given her sketchy biography, which indicates that her line in the plot, like that of the many montage characters, has served its purpose and come to an end (Dollenmayer 1988, 95). People in *Berlin Alexanderplatz* think that looking and going straight ahead are sufficient safeguards to protect them: "You can let me run along. Didn't you talk about feet and eyes? I've still got them all right. Nobody's chopped 'em off for me yet" (27), Franz says proudly as he comes to terms with his new freedom after being released from prison. His hubristic words resonate ominously as he first loses his arm and, then, Mieze is murdered.

No protective, loving space is available for people in *Berlin Alexanderplatz*: walking offers the alternative to being enclosed in dark, depressing, lonely rooms. The streets, like prostitutes, appear to substitute for domestic values, but instead, they end up robbing their walkers. The rambling characters in *Petersburg* and *Ulysses* likewise roam the streets of the city for want of a protective home. In the Irish and Russian novels, the central walking characters are at least at home when they look inside themselves. They comprehend their situation, and importantly, they have their memories of times past. Franz Biberkopf, however, is completely out of touch with life outside his immediate environment. He does not have any awareness of the history of his city, his nation, or his religion. The only form of culture available to him comes in the way of advertisements, the newspapers, the radio, and the "wisdom" of the streets.

Indeed, the primitive, proletarian inhabitants of the Alexanderplatz district resemble slaughter cattle; their naïveté results from losing touch with their own humanity. They are so alienated in the city that they can only perceive a most superficial sense of reality. Similar imagery of the city crowd features in both *Petersburg* and *Ulysses*. Bely's vision of the crowd as a caviar sandwich emphasizes passivity and helplessness as the individual disappears in the mass. In Bloom's stream of consciousness in the "Lestrygonians" chapter of *Ulysses*, the image of the cattle market arises: "Wretched brutes there at the cattlemarket waiting for the poleaxe to split their skulls open. Moo. Poor trembling calves. Meh. Staggering bob. Bubble and squeak. . . . Rawhead and bloody bones. Flayed glasseyed sheep hung from their haunches, sheepsnouts bloodypapered snivelling nosejam on sawdust" (8.723–27). Here, again, strong emphasis is placed on the ignorance of the animals who offer no resistance as they are about to be butchered; they are aware of each other in the crowd but do not understand the reason for being there. The image thus becomes a potent metaphor about the relationship between the city and the individuals.

In *Berlin Alexanderplatz*, incomprehension, resembling the animals in the slaughterhouse, accounts for the rash decision made by Gerner and Gusta, whose story is one of the "excrescences" of the novel. A hitherto "decent" lower-middle-class couple agree, in the hope of easy money, to let a gang of thieves use their flat for storing goods obtained by burgling the warehouse in the yard of the block where Gerner is the caretaker. The couple are the most immediate suspects and are caught by the police immediately, of course. Similarly "blind" is a young man in another montage insertion: "Then he got to know the present one in Hoppegarten, where she was out man-hunting. The same brand of woman as the first, only a bit cleverer. He doesn't notice anything when his girl-friend goes off every few days on a so-called business-trip" (160). Blindly, people apprehend dangers but never comprehend them. Glancing at Minna doing her shopping, the narrator notices: "In front of the market she buys something else from a wagon: a big flat flounder and a bag of camomile tea, you never can tell, you may need it any day" (130). Danger, like the potential illness to be cured with camomile tea, is never noticed where it lurks. Franz hums popular ballads which warn of "fate"; "Wait a while, my little beaver, soon will Haarmann come to you, with his little chopping cleaver, he'll make sausage out of you, wait a while, my little beaver, soon will Haarmann come to you" (388). Lacking the ability for introspection, Franz clearly does not see the analogy between himself and the "little beaver." After he finds out about Mieze's murder, he is in a daze, like slaughter animals when they smell blood. "The street-cars rattle along the streets, they are all going somewhere, but I don't know where to go," he muses. Like the young man betrayed by his girlfriend, or Gerner and Gusta, Franz feels the blow but is not fully aware of the nature of his condition. The montage episodes suggest that many in the uniform crowd have predicaments similar to Franz's because they are unable—like pigs about to be butchered—to resist the bad luck descending on them.

Chance meetings, gullibility, and deceit highlight Franz's Berlin life too. He cannot bear being indoors, in his dreary room, where he is unable to occupy himself. The three "blows" come to Franz from the city, yet he always rushes out into the street to immerse himself in its atmosphere. The city, however, is an abstraction; the concrete spaces are where people work, shop, eat, and, most significantly, where they are born, sleep, have sex, love, and hate. It is from the domestic space that people set out to create the metropolitan crowd in the streets. Döblin's city, like Bely's and Joyce's, is a compendium of homes:

[T]he cities which lie along the same line, Breslau, Liegnitz, Sommerfeld, Guben, Frankfort on the Oder, Berlin, the train passes through them from station to station, from the stations emerge the cities, the cities with their big and little streets. Berlin with Schweidnitzer Strasse, with the Grosse Ring of the Kaiser-Wilhelm Strasse, Kurfürstendamm, and everywhere are homes in which people are warming themselves, looking at each other with loving eyes, or sitting coldly next to each other; dirty dumps and dives where a man is playing the piano. (608)

The Alexanderplatz area—unlike upper-middle-class Berlin—is a dirty, dark maze of blocks of flats: "To the right and left are streets. House follows house along the streets. They are full of men and women from cellar to garret" (154). "Homeloving" characters like Bloom do not exist in *Berlin Alexanderplatz*. Bloom's memory of happiness is connected with the houses he occupied when he was younger. Even in 1904, he still has his Molly to go home to. In *Petersburg*, people are generally terrified within their walls. Nonetheless, Apollon Apollonovich feels secure in small enclosures like the toilet. He would like to live in a well-enclosed little room. In Döblin's novel, however, all experiences of domestic space in the long run tend to be unhappy. Thanks to the technique of the montage, we see how dozens of people, who do not even know, or know of, each other, experience similar misery in what is supposed to be their sheltering and protective domestic space. Döblin's Berliners seek their fortunes and happiness in public rather than in private places.

Franz opts to stay indoors only when he is at his lowest ebb. As he faces on his own a state of complete dejection, the invisible narrative voice alone shows some concern: "—Franz, for two weeks you haven't stirred out of your wretched room.... If you don't pull yourself together soon, you'll have to go to the poorhouse.... You don't let any air into your hole, you won't go to the barber, you're getting a full brown beard" (183). Many montage images reveal a general sense of frustration in the home. Such is the case with the "elderly woman": "He is a dashing man... but he is under forty and that's the trouble. When he comes home late, the old woman is still awake and unable to sleep for rage" (156). It twice happens to Franz's girlfriends that he goes away from "home" never to return. Lina waits for Franz with a present, a new sweater, but Franz does not come. Then Lina passes "twenty-four horrible hours" before starting to look for him. Cilly's experience is the same: "Franz laughed: 'Well, I'm off. Bye-bye, Cilly.' 'Bye-bye, Franzeken.' Then Franz went slowly down the four flights of stairs, and he never saw Cilly again" (268). In the "excrescences"— the elements of the montage—we read about the carpenter who is debarred from his home because of his ill wife, whose complaints the doctors fail to take seriously: "She needs her rest; at eight o'clock sharp . . . I've got to put out the lights. What can I do upstairs? That's what drives a man to the saloons, when a man's got a sick woman" (384–85). The doctors also accuse Ernst of feigning illness; this exacerbates his depression and he hangs himself in the cellar. No privacy is available indoors. The reputation and peace of mind of the homosexual man are ruined because the owners of his rented room peep through a hole as he is having sex with a boy, and subsequently, they report him to the police. The bed, as a nucleus of inner space, proves to be of great phenomenological importance in *Ulysses*. In *Petersburg*, too, the bed provides a border crossing for transitions into "astral" space, an alternative "reality." In *Berlin Alexanderplatz*, the bed is to be the locus where deception and self-deception are uncovered. As Franz lies in bed in a catatonic stupor in the Buch asylum, he has a cleansing vision allowing him to see his guilt and stupidity. But even earlier in the novel, Franz wakes up at night, soon before the fatal trip when he is pushed out of a speeding car and loses an arm. As he sits up in the bed, "[i]t's ice-cold in his room . . . Franz tosses about. Hatred of Reinhold weighs on him, wrangles with him. It penetrates the wooden door and wakes him up" (251–52).

The turning point of the novel occurs when Franz invites Reinhold, his undoer, to hide in the bed in which he and his girlfriend, Mieze, sleep. He wants Reinhold to spy on his domestic happiness. Reinhold overhears the unsuspecting Mieze's naive confession to Franz about fancying a younger man. Apart from betraying their intimacy, Franz also prepares the ground for Mieze's murder and, thus, his own destruction; the scandal and physical abuse that ensue give Reinhold the idea as to how he should proceed to make Franz suffer. Franz makes such a serious error not so much because he has no sense of decency, but rather because he has no sense of property and privacy, no inclination to domesticity. While Bloom loves the warm bed, his cat, and even the nymph on the painting above his bed, Franz is deprived of such experiences. He attempts to look for continuity in his life by fighting impermanence, but never succeeds.

The obvious way to evoke the experiences of bygone days is by finding the spaces of the past. Franz Biberkopf has no more immediate home than the city itself. When he recollects the past, he thinks of locations in Berlin: residences of some of his acquaintances and certain public locations like the "Alex." The trams moving about the city, following the same route day after day, offer Franz some sense of permanence too. Significantly, the title of the first section of the book is "On Car 41 into Town" (Durrani 1987, 146). After all his vicissitudes at the end of the novel, upon his return to the Alexanderplatz area, Franz takes comfort in the fact that the "[s]treet-cars are chock-full of people, all of them have something to do, the tickets still cost 20 pfennigs" (627). After his release from Tegel prison, on three occasions Franz visits Minna, the sister of the girlfriend he murdered. On the first visit, his seduction of Minna verges on rape; he succeeds in asserting his manhood only with the woman who somehow connects him to his younger self. His visits to Minna are forcefully terminated by her angry husband. Biberkopf also returns twice to the Jewish men in Dragonstrasse after his first visit on his way out of Tegel prison. At that time, they took him in temporarily and helped him come to appreciate his newly regained freedom in Berlin by telling him the story of Zannowich, whose life came to an abrupt end with his suicide in a prison cell. Like Biberkopf, he was thirty.

Franz appreciated the story because without it he would not have had the courage to assume the responsibility of freedom outside the prison. He liked it in jail because of the order and decorum that are necessarily and forcefully imposed on day-to-day life there. In prison, the basic aspects of domesticity, however meager, are provided: one receives food and a bed. After regaining his freedom, Franz faces constant difficulties earning an income by "decent" means to provide such things for his life. While still in prison, the option of remaining respectable after his release seemed a plausible one. Once in civilian life, however, Franz faces insurmountable difficulties in leading a crime-free existence. He is drawn to the streets and public places, where all his troubles start, because—for all his yearning for a home—he has none. He muses in one of his critical periods: "To bed, to bed, if you've got one, or if you haven't, you must all go to bed, to bed" (169).

Franz nostalgically returns to Tegel on two occasions when he faces a crisis. The prison, significantly, is located opposite a sanatorium. This is symbolic of Franz's fate: his "progress" leads him from Tegel at the beginning of the novel to the Buch mental asylum at the end. In the middle of his story, he spends time in a Magdeburg hospital, where they operate on him after his accident. Prisons and hospitals are alternative "homes" supplied by "civilization," the city, that is. They offer a shelter of sorts to those who, for some reason, fail to pursue urban life in the way expected of them. Mental illness and crime are rooted in an inability to "conquer" the city. In *Petersburg* people run away from homes where unhappiness lurks. People in *Berlin Alexanderplatz*, however, invite danger into their most intimate nooks. Franz leads a "friend," Lüders, to the home of a well-to-do widow; Lüders promptly robs Franz of the woman's "patronage."

The streets and public places are significant enough that they almost make the city appear as a personified figure. The topographical accuracy enables one to follow easily the movement of the story in the actual city, from square to square, from street corner to street corner. Since the characters do not wander into "fourth-dimensional" space in *Berlin Alexanderplatz*, we would not in any real-life reproduction of movement about the city even have to think of such obstacles as the "Circe" episode in *Ulysses* might pose; as was discussed in the previous chapter, three-dimensional movement here is thoroughly fused with movement in the "fourth dimension" of desires, memories, and fantasies.

The Alexanderplatz became the central point where the main tram lines of Berlin intersected. The city's "S-Bahn"—the elevated railway system—also had a station in the square and, in the 1920s, the building of the underground network, in particular that of the "Alexanderplatz" station, was well under way.[2] The city is personified in some of the quick glimpses that are interspersed throughout the novel; identifiably accurate urban details pile up with such rapidity that the reader senses the swift movement of vehicles and the rush of the crowd. The Rosenthaler Platz is "busily active" and the drilling machine keeps destroying to make room for new construction. It is as though the inanimate world were taking the initiative, not the people occupying it. Every time Franz overcomes a crisis and "reconquers" Berlin, it is the roofs, not Franz, that seem to slide, and the houses that seem to sway (Schoonover 1977, 202). The active voice suggests that the city is a live entity and it—rather than the people—takes charge of events. The anthropomorphous urban world shows outright hostility to its loyal son, Franz. When he makes futile attempts to find Reinhold after the announcement of Mieze's murder, the building in which Reinhold lives engages Franz in an ominous dialogue:

> The house bursts into laughter, as it sees him standing there. It would like to be able to move in order to collect its neighbors, so that the crosswise wing and the end wings could get a look at him. Here's a fellow with a wig and an artificial arm, a flaming fool, full of liquor, standing and jawing about something.
> "How do you do, lil' Biberkopf? This is November 22nd. Still rainy weather. Do you want to catch a cold? Wouldn't rather go to your beloved saloon and get a cognac? . . ."
> Then Franz Biberkopf works in the house one evening, he hides a gasoline can and a bottle.
> "Come out, are you hiding there, you snake, you stinking dog? You haven't got the nerve to come out, have you?"

The house: "Why are you calling him when he's not here? . . ."
"Give him up to me. It'll go bad with you otherwise."
"You and your 'it'll go bad with you.' Go home fellow. . . ." (547–48)

The city also distresses Franz by preventing him from developing attachments to places. The Alexanderplatz itself ideally represents the constant change and lack of permanence that are central issues in the novel:

> On the Alexanderplatz they go on fussing and bustling around. On Königstrasse, at the corner of Neue Friedrichstrasse, they want to pull down the house over the Salamander shoe-store. They are already pulling down the one next to it. Traffic beneath the Alex arch of the municipal railway becomes enormously difficult: they are building new pillars for the railway bridge; here you can look down a nicely walled shaft where the pillars put their feet. (416)

Clearly, Biberkopf's only sense of identity arises from being a Berliner. It is impossible to imagine him anywhere but in his Berlin. His life is intertwined with the Alexanderplatz, the Elsasserstrasse, the Rosenthalerplatz, and the surrounding areas: "He is back in Berlin. He breathes Berlin again. When he sees the houses on the Elsasser Strasse again, something stirs within him" (302). Inasmuch as Franz is frequently involved in illegal activities, he understandably wishes to minimize contacts with the authorities. He certainly spends no less of the narrated time in the streets than the walkers of *Ulysses*; for sure, walking is a more central concern here than in *Petersburg*. Nevertheless, Franz is least like a flâneur. Instead, he is a faceless walker in a crowd, one who can easily disappear. A capable metropolitan "badaud," Franz is very good at not being noticed in the street, even when he has only one arm. He knows how to don false identities, even false arms. He is eventually arrested only when he wants to call attention to himself. Franz's style of moving about town is certainly not in any way idiosyncratic. The people roaming the streets of Berlin are conspicuous solely by their lack of individuality: "The faces of the eastward wanderers are in no way different from those of the wanderers to the west, south, and north; moreover they exchange their roles, those who are now crossing the square towards Aschinger's may be seen an hour later in front of the empty Hahn Department Store" (221). For all his hubris and confidence, Franz is unable to understand the signs of the city (Scherpe 1989, 162). The sense of security with which he walks about the streets as the "man of the crowd" turns out to be completely false.

Franz feels safe when there are high walls around him. His balance is restored in prison and his mental turmoil is cured in the psychiatric ward; in both the prison and the hospital he is safely enveloped. When released, he feels that he has "conquered the city" as soon as he no longer fears that the roofs may skid or the asphalt move: "Biberkopf continued walking in a happy mood. Only here and there was he obliged to look at the pavement. He examined his steps and the nice firm asphalt. But then his glance slipped with a jerk up the house-fronts, examined them, made sure they were standing still and did not stir. . . . The roofs could slide down, . . . obliquely over the roof-tree, along the whole row" (165–66).

Of course, it is self-delusory to derive a feeling of protection simply from the fact that the houses do not collapse. His other source of false security is a naive belief—shared by many other Berliners—in the protection big crowds supposedly offer. As he visits the Jewish men upon his release from prison, one of them tells him: "Now, now, it's not going to be as bad as all that. You're not going to go under. Berlin is big. Where a thousand live, one more can also live" (9). When he gets used to moving about freely in Berlin again, Franz confidently hums a well-known tune from Engelbert Humperdinck's opera, *Hansel und Gretel*, and vaguely assumes that by being one of the multitude, he enjoys some sort of protection: "Thus let us start off merrily. We want to sing and move about: with our little hands going clap, clap, clap, our little feet going tap, tap, tap, moving to, moving fro, roundabout, and away we go. Franz Biberkopf Enters BERLIN" (50). Franz's choice of song from an opera based on the tale by the Grimm Brothers is ironical: *Hansel und Gretel* relates the story of naive children surrounded by an ominous world. The "wicked witch" figure in the tale invites comparisons with the Whore of Babylon. The witch in the tale does not succeed in killing the children by burning them in the oven; however, the allusion to *Hansel und Gretel* offers yet another image on the theme of massacring the innocent, as in the slaughterhouse or in Mieze's case.

Franz's hopes lie in his bodily strength and he assumes that one is safe on one's own as long as one's arm is strong. Indeed, he is at his best when, as a member of the Berlin crowd, he can perform socially useful activity: "On Brunnerstrasse, where they are excavating for the subway, a horse has fallen into the hole . . . Franz jumps into the hole with the firemen and helps pull the horse up. Meck, and everybody else is astonished at what Franz can do with his one arm" (328). Such confidence in physical strength is blind: as the slaughterhouse allegory recurs, it keeps suggesting that no matter how strong the bull is, he is butchered anyway when his time comes.

The fates of several unrelated inhabitants, who make up the city crowd, paint a very grim picture of poverty and alienation in an unsympathetic metropolis. Whilst he is vaguely aware of lurking dangers, and he does not understand the workings of human relations in the city, it never occurs to Franz not to trust the various people he accidentally comes across. He thinks that all his vicissitudes come about as a result of "accidents." Indeed, his method of making friends is the only one available to him: since he spends all his time in the street, without a steady job in a period of massive unemployment, his meetings all happen by chance. He accidentally meets Lüders; again, he accidentally meets Reinhold, who pushes him out of a speeding car. If it had not been for the accident, he would never have got in touch with his old friend, the prostitute Eva, who, in turn, introduces Franz to Mieze. It is also accidental, according to Franz, that he renews his relationship with Reinhold, who brings him and Mieze misery and destruction. Franz's blind trust in him is, again, akin to meek animals in the slaughterhouse who accept "fate."

The monteur-narrator, however, presents life in the city in such grim terms that any belief in accidents as the sole source of wide-scale unhappiness among Döblin's Berliners loses credibility: "Some women and girls are walking across Alexanderstrasse and the square, each carrying a fetus in her belly, protected by law. It is hot, and the women and girls are sweating outside, but the fetus within sits quietly in his corner, the temperature is just right for him as he walks across the Alexanderplatz, but many a fetus will fare badly later on; he'd better not laugh too soon" (503).

Such a melodramatic image of expressionistic gloom would be inconceivable in *Ulysses* which, in spite of its concern with weighty issues of human existence, still presents Dublin on a beautiful summer's day. In *Petersburg*, people go about the streets enveloped in fog and cold, moist air, but up above, the red rays of the sun are reflected in the turrets and spires of a city both mysterious and beautiful. Bely's novel conveys a definite sense of the countryside surrounding the city. In the interconnecting sets of symbols, the city's status is partially determined by its relationship with the hinterland, rural Russia. References to rural Ireland, Irish politics, religion, history, and folklore are interspersed throughout *Ulysses*. *Berlin Alexanderplatz*, however, reveals no awareness of the German provinces surrounding the capital. In Döblin's Berlin, be it summer or winter, the natural elements are always highly unpleasant. Sunshine is rarely mentioned in the novel. We hear a paean about the greatness of the sun immediately after the description of Reinhold pushing Franz under a speeding car in the dead of night: the effect, of course, is heavily ironical and suggests that the ways of the city are profoundly unnatural. Franz and many others are caught up in an urban world of quick fortunes and even quicker losses, construction and destruction, far removed from the established conventions of traditional life in the country. The weather is as unreasonably bad as Franz and the other Berliners are inexplicably insistent on living in the dark. The narrating voice explicitly draws attention to such an analogy: "[F]or what reason, I wonder, is it raining like that in August, the whole month simply swimming away from a fellow, it splashes off like nothin' on earth, for what reason does Franz go to see Reinhold of late and jaw and jaw about him" (424). A sense of powerlessness prevails: bad weather and a great deal of disconcerting news concerning the city and an invisible outside world floods over Döblin's Berliners. The question of "fate" is more than a thematic concern in *Berlin Alexanderplatz*: it is perceived as a force propelling human life (Bayerdorfer 1983, 152). The image of "Death"—the reaper—and the figure of "hubris" recur throughout the novel: the implied reader is told by the narrating voice in no uncertain terms that it is Biberkopf's boasting and pride that account for his demise (Dollenmayer 1988, 83).

Although the surrounding world of the city is incomprehensible to Franz throughout the book, at the very end, the narrative intimates that in some unspecified "collective," "we can defend ourselves against many other things," if not the "hail and storm" (634). The spiritual rebirth of a "new" Biberkopf at the end of the novel marks a transformation.[3] The essence of the "new" Biberkopf's wisdom is supposed to be that he now knows that the city can victimize him only as long as he is alone. After his final "blow," as he is gradually regaining consciousness, he realizes that he can now come to terms with the incomprehensible city if he joins the "community" of people tormented by the same malaise: "Much unhappiness comes from walking alone. When there are several, it's somewhat different. I must get the habit of listening to others, for what the others say concerns me, too. Then I learn who I am, and what I can undertake. Everywhere about me my battle is being fought, and I must beware, before I know I'm in the thick of it" (633). But with the exception of the jubilant tone of the final pages, the novel is the story of the "old" Biberkopf, and nobody around him seems to live the way the end of the book suggests one should. Walter Muschg proposed that the end of the novel had a Christian catharsis; he considered *Berlin Alexanderplatz* to be Döblin's first Christian novel (Kreutzer 1970, 115). It has also been postulated that the end of the novel shows that Franz Biberkopf has finally been integrated into society. But it is difficult to evaluate the "new" Biberkopf (a gatekeeper in a medium-size factory); no textual evidence justifies claims that he is redeemed by the end of his story or that the novel ends on an optimistic note (Durrani 1987, 142–44). Walter Benjamin suggests that Biberkopf's social progress takes him from pimp to petty bourgeois during the course of the events in the novel (Prangel 1975, 112). However, no real evidence is available to substantiate this claim. True enough, the "new Biberkopf" does not womanize upon his final return to Berlin: his sexuality—stormy relationships with girlfriends, mingled with possible latent homosexuality—landed him in trouble in the past. But the same whoop we heard at the beginning of the novel is repeated upon his final return: "Now Biberkopf is back again: your Biberkopf is back again" (624). Without any evidence supporting the contrary, it is a fair assumption that Biberkopf's sexual conduct will remain the same as before and the lower-middle-class "decency" will stay as unattainable as ever. Furthermore, even if Franz at the end of the novel may be uninterested in joining the "marching men"—Nazis or Communists—he is most unlikely to be able to maintain neutrality.

The didactic structure of the novel is parodistic and the ending offers a mock catharsis. Whereas Bely ends his novel on a solemn note, Joyce does not direct narrating voices toward an authorial resolution of the conflict. In the last chapter of *Ulysses*, "Penelope," the narrative voice is completely extinct, which, of course, could never occur in *Berlin Alexanderplatz*. Instead, the juxtaposition of a variety of narrative strands creates a sense of parody and so does the set of didactic references to the closure-bound structure of the epic. As in a fairy tale, Franz faces three challenges and "fails" three times with increasing force. However, the three trials do not lead to the resolution of the conflict. The ending is hardly less problematic than the beginning: no answers have been found to the moral and social problems that the novel had raised (Dollenmayer 1988, 2). The jubilant tone of the narration raises false expectations of a closure for the implied reader; he or she has also been falsely led to expect a "constructive" story, a *Bildungsroman*.[4] We read about a little girl in one of the montage segments: she is emigrating to America and the narrator assures us that if she is a "good little girl," all will be well. Readers who take such trite and superficial "wisdom" at face value blind themselves to the implications of the novel's ending: the clichéd bourgeois mores of honesty and decency are applied to no avail in a destructive and corrupt society. The city offers no solution to Biberkopf; similarly, the city resolves nothing for the characters of *Petersburg* or *Ulysses* either.

Throughout Franz's wanderings, a narrative voice seems to accompany him, focusing on his thoughts and actions. This voice keeps reminding Franz of his promise to lead a "decent" life; furthermore, it points out (in vain) to Franz the "Whore of Babylon" who is after him. Because of his low level of education, this narrating persona resembles the protagonist, and it is fair to assume that the characteristic Berlin "logic" of the storyteller's thinking could be Franz's own. According to this logic, "high culture"—mythology and literature—and the folk wisdom of proverbs alike can be turned around in such a way as to justify criminal activity and irresponsible behavior. The heading "Ill-gotten gain thrives" is the narrator's, but it also reflects Franz's frame of mind. When we read about Mieze's violent murder at Reinhold's hands, the narrating voice keeps repeating the words of Ecclesiastes: "To everything its season, to everything, everything" (Schoonover 1977, 102; Mahlendorf 1986, 104). One might wonder, by whose standards can there be a proper time for violent murder? Undoubtedly, Mieze's death devastates Franz, but the misappropriated quotation from Ecclesiastes suggests that he is reluctant to admit partial responsibility for the murder Reinhold commits: he lied to Mieze about Reinhold and he also offered the means for Reinhold's destructive action by exposing both Mieze's and his own vulnerability. In the many passages of the montage that are introduced into the plot, the Job-character, like Ecclesiastes, shows affinities with Franz. Resembling Franz at the Buch Sanatorium, Job does not want to be cured because recovery would force him to assume responsibility for the consequences of being ignorant and weak. Franz's unjustifiable confidence in himself is a result of the courage he gains from his bodily strength. Job, paralleling Franz, is also reluctant to come to terms with his weakness.

To throw light on what the people of Alexanderplatz do not comprehend, the narrator introduces a complex framework of biblical, mythological, and allegorical references. These point to parallels between life in the past and life in modern Berlin, but they do not add a temporal dimension, nor do they produce a "fourth dimension" in the novel. Rather, they are at the service of some implied social "message" that has to do with the actual Berlin of the late 1920s. In *Petersburg* no such parallels are available; city and individual both originate in a higher realm. The concept of parallelism is, in fact, irrelevant. The way for people to begin to understand is to penetrate behind the surface: it is the astral walk that leads to a transcendental realm wherein humans can see truth, as generated by the consciousness of the text. Such a truth in *Ulysses* is illuminated by epiphanies that arise as a result of the juxtaposition of many naturalistic details. In their minds, the walkers cross the boundaries between the "here and now," the mythical, and the historical. Transcendence, in this sense, does not occur in *Berlin Alexanderplatz*. Bely's symbols and Joyce's epiphanies yield their place to allegories and debunking, ironical effects. Accounts of human life in the city are placed alongside the passages from Greek mythology and the Bible (Ziolkowski 1969, 109). The ironical narrating voice tells the story of Abraham and Isaac in the oversimplifying and complacent manner of the petit bourgeois Berliner.

Come nearer. Is it the Lord God's will? Uphill, downhill, I have risen so early. You will not play the coward? I know, I know, I know! What do you know, my son? Take the knife to me, wait; I will turn my collar back so that my neck may be quite free. You seem to know something. You must will it and I must will it, and thus we will both accomplish it, and then the Lord will call and we will hear him call: Cease!! Yes, come, offer your neck. There! I am not afraid, I do it with joy. Uphill, downhill, long valleys, there, take the knife to me and begin to cut! I shall not cry out. (392)

Thus, the story of Abraham and Isaac turns into a comedy (Elm 1991, 125). The tragedy of Agamemnon and Clytemnestra is also narrated in *Berlin Alexanderplatz* in a stylistic pastiche mixing the lofty discourse with Berlin slang. The storytelling voice refers to Clytemnestra as a "cold-blooded beast" who "does in her husband." Thus, the classical myth, in its complex portrayal of human desires and profound awareness of the tragic limitations of human ambition, integrates the intellectual level of uneducated twentieth-century city dwellers whose sensitivity and reason have largely been replaced by consumerism. Myth appears in a different light in both Bely and Joyce. Bely attempts to create an overtly mythopoeic text whilst Joyce's parody regards legends of the past and the present of Dubliners in each other's light. Döblin's ironical handling, however, debunks them both.

The ignorance of Döblin's sauntering Berliners is further emphasized by the narrator's illustration of their smug functionality. Like all the others, Franz dismisses the collective human experience handed down in myth, history, art, and literature. The narrator makes his point by remarking that Orestes is pursued by the Furies, but Franz is not; he walks about in a leisurely way and sits in cafes. The only dimension Berliners in the novel recognize is the physical, tangible one. Döblin's novel, unlike *Ulysses* or *Petersburg*, does not utilize the "fourth-dimensional" potential of characters, like Reinhold, for example: the narrative hints merely at sexual and mental imbalance as an explanation for Reinhold's cruelty. Bely's and Joyce's characters who are not fully or obviously human, like M'Intosh in *Ulysses* or Shishnarfne and the Bronze Horseman in *Petersburg*, feature in the main plot and not in montage-like side plots to which the allegorical figures of *Berlin Alexanderplatz* are relegated.

Two such figures follow Franz: the Whore of Babylon and Death. The more Franz becomes involved with Reinhold, the greater the significance of the Whore is: she laughs as Franz sinks deeper and deeper. The Whore of Babylon, together with the symbols of the slaughterhouse, represents the inhumanity of the city; the narrative here draws on the imagery of the book of Revelation.

The Whore is a female figure riding a diabolical scarlet-colored beast with seven heads and ten horns. Like the houses, she laughs at Franz as she witnesses his undoing: she makes her appearance at such critical junctures as when Franz cannot resist the urge to resume his "friendship" with Reinhold. The other figure, Death, is the source of the unidentified "voice" Franz keeps hearing, first before his involvement with Lüders, then before his involvement with Reinhold. As Death tells the unconscious Franz—who is being cured in the asylum—that he sent him "blows" for his education, the voice we hear seems to be at one with the proselytizing narrator. Franz's subconscious battle is allegorical because it is designed to make a moral point. The didacticism that the presence of the allegorical figures brings forth is again restrained, however, by the chorus of voices in the plural text. The heteroglot discourse, just as in *Ulysses* and *Petersburg*, prevails over the authority of the individual voice. Even Death, the allegorical figure that carries the greatest weight within the didactic framework, speaks in an unmistakably Berlin "underworld" dialect: "You didn't open your eyes, you poor fool! You've been blind, and pretty cocky at that, turning your nose up at the world" (604). Apart from the Berlin dialect, which typifies the speech of most of the characters as we hear them in dialogues and interior monologues, a variety of narrating voices in standard high German, Old Testamental lamentation, the style of matter-of-fact reporting, and the language of documentaries resound throughout the text (Ziolkowski 1969, 110). The narrative, filled with speech fragments from the Berlin street, songs and proverbs, gossip and news, functions as a vast stream of consciousness of the faceless crowd (Titche 1971, 129). In the polyphonous choir, the montage segments and also Franz's story lose their individuality and the voice of Döblin's Berlin resonates (Elm 1991, 129; Scherpe 1989, 170), which inevitably creates a parodistic effect. Parody in Joyce pervades all levels; he views "low" and "high" discourse as of equal value in the human context. In *Petersburg* parody and myth are kept separate. Unlike Franz Biberkopf, Nikolai Apollonovich resolves never to walk with other people in cities: he decides to live the life of a social outcast. The impact of *Ulysses* also makes us cautious about too optimistic an evaluation of the potential of the urban crowd as a beneficial force.

As with *Ulysses*, references invite Döblin's readers to contemplate whether the texts to which the novel alludes merit any higher authority than the narrative of *Berlin Alexanderplatz*. Belief in the "functionality" of modern times reinforces the idea in the final pages that society is a force whose values are capable of standing against "Nature" and "fate." Franz and the narrator chant their message like a Salvation Army preacher or a doctrinaire socialist. For all this, however, their advocating words stand in a dialogic relationship with all those other voices that can lead an existence free of the intentions of the narrator's consciousness. Thus, the final note of *Berlin Alexanderplatz* is dissipated in the modern linguistic fabric of the novel, the "metropolis text" (Scherpe 1989, 164); we do not have to accept the verdict of the narrative, but are free to make sense of the text as we, the readers, produce it for ourselves.

Döblin's theoretical statements about the effect of collage or montage point to significant affinities with Joyce's and Bely's methods. Sixteen years before writing *Berlin Alexanderplatz*, Döblin had already talked about a "Kinostil" to be used in fiction to counteract and challenge the self-assured narratorial "analysis" of psychological motives (Dollenmayer 1988, 319). Collage or montage in these three novels is achieved by using the perspective of the walker. As he roams the streets, he is exposed to the flotsam and jetsam of urban life—a veritable chaos of phenomena—which, when thrown together, begin to make sense. Readers of *Petersburg, Ulysses* and *Berlin Alexanderplatz* wander about the text, much as the characters and the narrators of the stories roam the city. Readers can rearrange the seemingly unconnected pieces of trivia, as they wander back and forth in the text. Thus, they discover relationships that are not, and cannot be, fully explained by some all-knowing consciousness, even if, as in *Berlin Alexanderplatz*, a strong—albeit ironical—authorial intention is clearly present.

The walkers in all three novels wander about the metropolis in search of the "substance" that is missing from their lives. The city does not offer them any order in the chaos; it provides as little comfort as does the enclosed, domestic space from which they hurry away. The complexity of the city is ultimately bound to be beyond the grasp of any walker, be he as ignorant as a Franz Biberkopf, as practical as a Leopold Bloom, as sensitive as a Nikolai Ableukhov, or as intelligent and artistic as a Stephen Dedalus. The plurality of experience in the text, however, arises from what all the walkers and storytellers see, think, and feel as they walk about. This offers a remarkable insight into the nature of life in the metropolis and even into the "identity" of a particular city. The reader can establish one of several patterns of coherence in the maze of the modern novel and the modern city and can, thus, enjoy a perspective whose completeness in "real life" is never available to a single viewer, however good his or her vision.

Conclusion

In all the arts, it is, perhaps, the modernist novel about the city that creates the most profound image of life at the beginning of the twentieth century. The viewpoint of the reader approximates to that of the rambling characters. Topography and mythology, past and present, the concrete city and the city of the mind all merge. The respective experiences of Petersburg, Dublin, and Berlin in these novels produce a general statement about the city as a metaphor of human life. In the epilogue of *Petersburg* we learn that Cairo, built on the ruins of ancient Egypt, evokes disgust in Nikolai Apollonovich; the montage projects troubled images of distant cities in *Berlin Alexanderplatz*, and here, as in *Ulysses*, the idea of Babylon burdens the novel's consciousness. Preoccupation with the transitory nature of civilizations—past and present—and with death and the dead dominates these texts, whose pages, however, are also filled with an unprecedented sense of mobility, colors, and constructive and destructive technology, in short, the phenomenon of the "modern." This seeming contradiction is also apparent in the endings of the three novels, each of which concludes without closure: for all their losses, the "peripatetic" characters ramble on toward a highly uncertain future. The "faith" that Bely's Nikolai Apollonovich has found is hardly more convincing as a guarantee of happiness than Franz Biberkopf's new "wisdom," according to which he must walk with "others" and not on his own. As Stephen Dedalus in *Ulysses* leaves Bloom in the small hours to face a new day, it remains as uncertain whether on 17 June any of his problems will be resolved as whether Molly will actually bring Bloom his breakfast in bed.

Even as characters keep searching for knowledge, truth, or happiness within the maze of signs that comprises the urban world, the themes of hopelessness, homelessness, and impotence gain prominence. Characters believe that they know, and belong to, their urban environment, but this assumption is false and leads to an ultimate conflict between citizens and their city. As a result, individuals fail to function as constructive members of their society, and in addition, they also fail as lovers, parents, sons, or daughters.

In each novel the atmosphere is tense, but particularly so in *Petersburg*, to which Volker Klotz aptly referred as the "explosive city" (1969). The history of Russia in the twentieth century certainly proves that Bely was justified in presenting the darkest image among the three novels both of city and civilization. One year after *Petersburg* was published, the revolution of October 1917 turned Russia into the oppressive Soviet state that more than confirmed some of the dark concerns that inform the novel. It is, indeed, no accident that, of all European cities, Petersburg, Dublin, and Berlin became the protagonists of the most influential urban novels. In each capital, changes were forthcoming that, even by the standards of twentieth-century Europe, were unusually severe. Each city was to undergo the greatest crisis of identity in its history. Visitors to Dublin, wishing to follow in the footsteps of Stephen Dedalus and Leopold Bloom, will need to relearn the names of streets and places. Dublin as capital of the Irish Republic has a different establishment and different political realities. It is, in fact, a city in a different country.

This is also the case in St. Petersburg and Berlin. The Russian city ceased to be the capital in the wake of the Bolshevik revolution. Furthermore, as early as during World War I, it was renamed Petrograd, which, no doubt, sounded less Germanic than the city's original name. Shortly after Lenin's death, the Soviets changed Petrograd to Leningrad. Some seven decades later, after the fall of the Soviets, the city was called St. Petersburg again. For the best part of seventy years, readers of Bely would have failed to find the English Embankment or Senate Square on any official map. Today, however, places have been given back their original names. Many Russians in the 1990s are trying to undo the effects of the past seventy-five years of communist rule as they attempt to re-create the spaces of the past by "de-sovietizing" them.

This is clearly not so in Dublin: Kingstown and Sackville Street firmly belong to the past and few people would like them to be called again by their old names. Yet, notwithstanding the obvious lack of nostalgia in Dublin for the imperial past, the spirit of Joyce's city is far better preserved here than that of Bely's city in St. Petersburg. The reason that Döblin's Berlin is forever lost, if not forgotten by Berliners, is different. Primarily, districts such as Alexanderplatz and Tegel were completely destroyed by bombing toward the end of World War II. We could not reenact Franz Biberkopf's wanderings today because many of the streets, squares, bridges, and department stores have disappeared, and their places are occupied by a city with changed looks and a different mentality. Berlin not only ceased to exist as the German capital, but it also housed two countries and two cities for four decades, and for much of that time, a wall, fortified by East German guards, watchtowers, minefields, and dogs, physically separated West from East.

Bely, Joyce, and Döblin capture the European city at a time when the relationships between the human subject, the city, and society have reached an insoluble tension: this not only marks the end of the flâneur's relatively uncomplicated joy of walking about in his environment but also heralds the end of a form of urban life that has evolved during the course of several hundred years. And yet, when we read the three novels, the ghost cities of bygone days are thrown into relief with rare vitality. They convey a sense of eternity that very few other places in fiction have. The literary art that evokes them has been more powerful than history, crushing symbolical and real walls alike. More so than the authors, their narrators, or characters, it is the readers of these books who can make a real *nostos*, conquering time and space.

Notes

1. The Emergence of the Modernist City Novel and Its Peripatetic Hero

1. The literary representation of Berlin differs from that of prominent nineteenth-century capitals. Novels focusing on the German capital appear only at the turn of the twentieth century when Berlin—a conglomeration of small towns—becomes a city similar in size and importance to London or Paris.

2. Presumably the sad spectacle of the suffering city informs the "immortal verses" of Count Khvostov in Pushkin's "Bronze Horseman." While Pushkin's irony about his minor fellow poet is apparent, it is still interesting that it is the figure of a poet that is captured standing alone, observing the tragedy and devastation of the previous day: the crowd of builders, merchants, and civil servants are too busy considering the opportunities of rebuilding to have time to ponder upon the human suffering in the wake of the flood.

2. Knights and Unicorns: The Walkers of *Petersburg*

1. *Petersburg* was published in five editions during the author's life. The third of these is the 1916 "Sirin" edition, which marked the book's first appearance in separate form. In 1916, Bely started to revise the text for a German translation to appear in 1919, and he kept on revising the text for a Russian edition to be published in Berlin in 1922. Unless otherwise stated, all citations from *Petersburg* are followed by page numbers, referring to Andrei Bely's *Petersburg*, translated, annotated, and introduced by Robert A. Maguire and John E. Malmstad (Bloomington: Indiana University Press, 1978). Maguire and Malmstad translated the 1922 Russian edition. For a variety of reasons, the 1922 edition is not automatically accepted as the canonical text (Elsworth 1983, 115). When the translation by Maguire and Malmstad skips passages that appear in the 1916 edition but not in the 1922 edition, I have used my own translation of the 1916 version. In these instances, quotations are followed by the Russian title of the novel, *Peterburg*, and the page numbers refer to the 1981 Soviet reprint of the 1916 edition (Moscow: Izdatel'stvo Nauka, 1981).

2. In *Words and Music in the Novels of Andrei Bely*, Ada Steinberg studies the difference between the polyphonic techniques of Bely and Dostoevsky. Unlike Dostoevsky, Bely constantly interferes with his characters' self-expression, not allowing them to speak

for themselves. Bely's polyphony resides "in ramified and multifaceted symbolism. . ." (1981, 245).

3. Both Anna Petrovna, Nikolai's mother, and Sofia Petrovna, with whom Nikolai is in love, have the patronymic "Petrovna," literally "Peter's daughter." They are each involved in unhappy relationships with the Ableukhov father and son, respectively. Peter the Great, the symbolic "father" of them all, plays a crucial role in what Bely sees as "cerebral play": the city arose from his consciousness. The city embodies all aspects of Peter's life, including marital trouble, betrayal, and hatred between father and son.

4. The Russian sound "y" does not exist in English. In order to evoke a similar effect, Maguire and Malmstad used the sound "sh" in their translation: "All words with 'sh' are outrageously trivial. 'S' isn't like that. 'S-s-s': sky, concept, crystal. The sound 's-s-s' evokes in me the image of the curve of an eagle's beak. But words with 'sh' are trivial. For example: the word *fish*. Listen: *fi-sh-sh-sh*. . . : something slimy: mu*sh*, something shapeless: ra*sh*, something diseased" (26; italics in the original).

5. Lippanchenko is likened to a rhinoceros at one place in the text (161). Maria Carlson notes that the unicorn is the Eastern ancestor of the rhinoceros (1980, 163).

6. While his surname amalgamates the Tatar name Ab-Lai with the Russian ending "ukhov," and thus alludes to his Eastern origins, Senator Ableukhov supports the establishment, in other words, Peter's efforts to raise the "wall." The metaphorical attempt to build "walls" has important classical associations (Barta 1991–92, 34).

7. In his "Memoirs," Bely talks about his "scissors problem," referring to his trauma as a child, torn between parents with contradicting personalities. He suffered from a feeling of "guiltless guilt" for trying to favor one of his parents over the other. This led him to identify with Christ. The motif of the innocent victim appears in all his novels, particularly in *The Baptized Chinaman* and *Kotik Letaev* (Alexandrov 1985, 37).

3. *Ulysses*: **The City of the Wandering Aengus and the Wandering Jew**

1. All quotations from the novel will be followed by the number of the chapter and the numbers of the quoted lines. Quotations are from James Joyce's *Ulysses*, The Corrected Text, ed. Hans Walter Gabler (New York: Vintage Books, 1986).

2. Angus Og (Angus the Young) was the god of beauty, youth, love, and maidens in Irish mythology. Mulligan presumably refers to Yeats' poem, "The Song of Wandering Aengus," which appeared in *The Wind among Reeds* (1899). Oliver Gogarty, Mulligan's real-life prototype, actually did call Joyce by this name (Thornton 1982, 216).

3. In addition to possessing a symbolic surname, Stephen's given name also has symbolic significance: it alludes to St. Stephen, the first Christian martyr who was persecuted by Greek-speaking Jews in Jerusalem. Of course, Stephen is Irish whereas, it is believed, St. Stephen was a Hellenist of foreign descent. Stephen projects the image of himself as a lonely outsider even as he contemplates his ancestors: "Then from the starving cagework city a horde of jerkined dwarfs, my people, with flayers' knives, running, scaling, hacking in green blubbery whalemeat. Famine, plague and slaughters. Their blood is in me, their lusts my waves. I moved among them on the frozen Liffey,

that I, a *changeling*, among the spluttering resin fires. *I spoke to no-one: none to me* (3.304–9; emphasis mine).

4. The conflict in *The Odyssey* has its genesis in the sea. Poseidon is Odysseus' chief adversary. Odysseus suffers shipwreck, and the sea keeps him away from Ithaca and his family. Telemakhos persistently fails to find his father at sea. Bloom contemplates the dangers awaiting the castaway: "Hanging on to a plank or astride of a beam for grim life, lifebelt round him, gulping salt water, and that's the last of his nibs till the sharks catch hold of him" (13.1160–62).

5. Robert Emmet was the leader of a group of United Irishmen in an unsuccessful rebellion on 23 July 1803. He was executed on 20 September 1803 at the age of twenty-five. The year 1903, the one preceding *Ulysses*, commemorated the one hundredth anniversary of the event. This accounts for the display of Emmet's portrait in a shop window.

6. Brian Boru defeated the Danes in the battle of Clontarf in 1014 but was killed by a Dane after the battle even as he was praying in his tent.

4. Walking in the Shadow of Death: *Berlin Alexanderplatz*

1. Quotations from *Berlin Alexanderplatz* will be followed by page numbers in parentheses, which refer to Eugene Jolas's translation (New York: Frederick Ungar Publishing Co., 1983).

2. Walter Benjamin writes in his article "Krisis des Romans: Zu Döblins *Berlin Alexanderplatz*": "Why is it called 'Berlin Alexanderplatz' with 'The Story of Franz Biberkopf' as a mere subtitle? What is the Alexanderplatz in Berlin? It is the place where, for two years, the most violent changes have been taking place; excavators and rams have been working without interruption; the ground has been shaking from their jolts, from the columns of buses and the trains of the underground; where the backyards of the Georgenkircheplatz have been opened up, uncovering the intestines of the metropolis deeper than anywhere else, and where districts from the nineties have remained quieter than anywhere else, in untouched labyrinths around the Marsiliusstrasse (where the clerks from the Foreigners' Police live, crammed into a tenement house) and Kaiserstrasse (where the whores act out their evening routine). This is no industrial area; trading comes first; the world of the petit bourgeois" (cited in Prangel 1975, 111; my translation).

3. The rebirth motif alludes to the New Testament and also to the "novus homo" of the late Roman Republic. This was a term used for the first man in the family to enter the Senate. Even if he himself occupied an insignificant role in the Senate, his descendants could attain higher ranks. The Christian idea of rebirth is similar. Christ, the *novus homo*, had, through his sufferings, made it possible for his descendants to be free of sin. In 6.6 of the Epistle of Paul to the Romans, we read: "being aware of this, that our self was crucified with him, so that the power of the sin-controlled body might be done away with and we should no longer be slaves of sin."

4. Döblin's comments about his novel seem to suggest a far more simplistic text than what he actually produces. He refers to a conventional closure, which, in my opinion, is absent from the novel. The story of Franz ends with a projection of a possible but, I would like to suggest, improbable future. He argues: "My new novel is entitled 'Berlin Alexanderplatz' and it concerns a man who, having been released from prison, tries to find a new life. After being thrown about, he finally realizes that what really matters is not to be a so-called decent person but, instead, to find the right companions. This realization helps him find himself again. Through his commitment to his new environment, he finds confidence in life again" (Cited in Prangel 1975, 41; my translation).

Bibliography

Primary Sources

Addison, Joseph, and Richard Steele. 1832. *The Spectator.* Vol. 1. Philadelphia: J. J. Woodward.

Baudelaire, Charles. 1947. *Paris Spleen.* Trans. Louise Varese. New York: New Directions.

Bely, Andrei. 1910. *Simvolizm: kniga statei* (Symbolism: a volume of articles). Moscow: Musaget.

———. 1978. *Petersburg.* Trans. Robert A. Maguire and John E. Malmstad. Bloomington: Indiana University Press.

———. 1981. *Peterburg.* Moscow: Izdatel'stvo Nauka.

———. 1986. *Selected Essays of Andrei Bely.* Ed. and trans. Steven Cassedy. Berkeley: University of California Press.

Dickens, Charles. 1965. *The Letters of Charles Dickens.* Vol. 4. Ed. Madeline House and Graham Storey. Oxford: Oxford University Press.

Döblin, Alfred. 1980. *Berlin Alexanderplatz.* Munich: Deutscher Taschenbuch Verlag GmbH und Co. KG.

———. 1983. *Berlin Alexanderplatz.* Trans. Eugene Jolas. New York: Frederick Ungar Publishing Co.

Dostoevsky, Fyodor. 1968. *White Nights.* Trans. David Magarshack. In *Great Short Works of Fyodor Dostoevsky.* New York: Harper and Row.

———. 1980. *Crime and Punishment.* Trans. Sidney Monas. New York: Signet.

Gogol, Nikolai. 1945. *Tales from Gogol.* Trans. Rosa Portnova. London: Sylvan Press.

Heine, Heinrich. 1983. *The Works of Heinrich Heine.* Trans. Charles Godfrey Leland. New York: Croscup and Streling Company.

Joyce, James. 1965. *A Portrait of the Artist as a Young Man.* New York: The Viking Press.

———. 1966. *Letters of James Joyce,* 2 vols. Ed. Richard Ellmann. New York: Viking Press.

———. 1986. *Ulysses.* Ed. Hans Walter Gabler with Wolfhard Steppe and Claus Melchior. New York: Vintage Books.

Pushkin, Aleksandr S. 1982. *The Bronze Horseman.* Trans. D. M. Thomas. New York: Viking Press.

Rhys, Jean. 1970. *Good Morning, Midnight*. New York: Harper and Row.
Woolf, Virginia. 1964. *Mrs Dalloway*. Harmondsworth, Middlesex: Penguin Books.

Secondary Sources

Ahearn, Edward J. 1989. "London and Dublin." *Marx and Modern Fiction*. New Haven: Yale University Press, 76–118.
Alexandrov, Vladimir E. 1982. "Unicorn Impaling a Knight: The Transcendent and Man in Andrei Bely's *Petersburg*." *Canadian American Slavic Studies* 16: 1–44.
———. *Andrei Bely*. 1985. Cambridge: Harvard University Press.
Alter, Robert. 1975. *The Novel as a Self-Conscious Genre*. Berkeley: University of California Press.
Anschuetz, Carol. 1983A. "Bely's *Petersburg* and the End of the Russian Novel." In *The Russian Novel from Pushkin to Pasternak*. Ed. John Garrard. New Haven: Yale University Press, 125–53.
———. 1983B. "Dostoevskij and Belyj's *Petersburg*." In *Dostojevskij und die Literatur*. Ed. Hans Rothe. Cologne: Bohlau Verlag, 251–63.
Babieva, I. R. 1993. "K voprosu o tipe romana nachala XX veka: *Peterburg* Belogo i *Uliss* Dzhoisa" (Concerning the question of the novel at the beginning of the twentieth century: *Petersburg* by Bely and *Ulysses* by Joyce). In *Nachalo: Sbornik rabot molodykh uchyonnykh*. Vol 2. Ed. T.A. Kasatkina. Moscow: Nasledie, 122–35.
Bachelard, Gaston. 1964. *The Poetics of Space*. Trans. Maria Jolas. Boston: Beacon Press.
Bakhtin, Mikhail. 1981. "Discourse in the Novel." *The Dialogic Imagination*. Ed. Michael Holquist. Trans. Caryl Emerson and Michael Holquist. Austin: University of Texas Press, 259–422.
Bance, Alan P. 1982. "Alfred Döblin's *Berlin Alexanderplatz* and Literary Modernism." In *Weimar Germany: Writers and Politics*. Ed. Alan P. Bance. Edinburgh: Scottish Academic Press Ltd., 53–64.
Banjamin, Milica. 1983. "Of Dreams, Phantoms, and Places: Andrei Bely's *Petersburg*." *International Fiction Review* 10, no. 2: 98–103.
Barrow, Craig Wallace. 1980. *Montage in James Joyce's "Ulysses"*. Madrid: Studia Humanitatis.
Barta, Peter I. 1986A. "Vision and Imagery in Blok's 'The Stranger,' Eliot's 'Rhapsody on a Windy Night' and Heym's 'Die Dämonen der Städte.'" *Studies in English and American* 6: 5–13.
———. 1986B. "The Apollonian and the Dionysian in Andrei Bely's *Petersburg*." *Studia Slavica* 32: 253–61.
———. 1987. "The Thematic and Structural Significance of Walking in the Modernist Urban Novel." Diss. University of Illinois.
———. 1988. "The Search for Father." *Dictionary of Literary Themes and Motifs*. Ed. Jean-Charles Seigneuret. New York: Greenwood Press, 1141–47.
———. 1990. "The Treatment of the Fourth Dimension in the Modernist City Novel." In *Spaces and Boundaries*. Vol. 3. *Proceedings of the XIIth Congress of the Interna-*

tional Comparative Literature Association. Ed. Roger Bauer. Munich: Iudicium Verlag, 210–15.

———. 1991–92. "Nietzschean Masks and the Classical Apollo in Andrei Bely's *Petersburg.*" *Studia Slavica* 37: 31–48.

Barthes, Roland. 1977. *Image-Music-Text.* New York: Hill and Wang.

Bater, James H. 1976. *St. Petersburg: Industrialization and Change.* Montreal: McGill University Press.

Bayerdorfer, Hans-Peter. 1983. "Alfred Döblin: *Berlin Alexanderplatz* (1929)." In *Deutsche Roman des 20 Jahrhunderts.* Ed. Paul Michael Lutzeler. Königstein: Athenaum, 148–66.

Benjamin, Walter. 1966. "Krisis des Romans: Zu Döblins *Alexanderplatz*" (The crisis of the novel: On Döblin's *Alexanderplatz*). *Angelus Novus: Ausgewählte Schriften.* Vol. 2. Frankfurt/M: Suhrkamp, 437–43.

———. 1969. *Illuminations.* Trans. Harry Zahn. Ed. Hannah Arndt. New York: Schocken Books.

———. 1972. *Gesammelte Schriften* (Collected writings) Vol. 5. Eds. Rolf Tredemann and Hermann Schweppenhauser. Frankfurt/M: Suhrkamp Verlag.

———. 1973. *Charles Baudelaire: A Lyric Poet in the Era of High Capitalism.* Trans. Harry Zahn. London, New Left Books.

———. 1978. *Reflections: Essays, Aphorisms, Autobiographical Writings.* Trans. Edmund Jephcott. Ed. Peter Demetz. New York: Harcourt Brace Jovanovich.

Bennett, Virginia. 1980. "Echoes of Friedrich Nietzsche's *The Birth of Tragedy* in Andrei Bely's *Petersburg.*" *Germano-Slavica* 3: 243–59.

Benstock, Bernard. 1970. "*Ulysses*: The Making of an Irish Myth." *Approaches to Ulysses.* Eds. Bernard Benstock and Thomas Staley. Pittsburgh: University of Pittsburgh Press.

———. 1972. "*Ulysses* without Dublin." *James Joyce Quarterly* 10, no. 1: 90–117.

———. 1982. *The Seventh of Joyce.* Bloomington: Indiana University Press.

———. 1985. *Critical Essays on James Joyce.* Boston: G. K. Hall.

———. 1985. *James Joyce.* New York: Frederick Ungar Publishing Co.

———, ed. 1988. *The Augmented Ninth.* Syracuse: Syracuse University Press.

Benstock, Bernard, and Suheil Badi Bushrui, Eds. 1982. *James Joyce: An International Perspective.* Gerrards Cross, Bucks.: Colin Smythe Ltd.

Benstock, Shari. 1975. "*Ulysses* as Ghoststory." *James Joyce Quarterly* 12, no. 4: 396–413.

———. 1988. "City Spaces and Women's Places in Joyce's Dublin." In *The Augmented Ninth.* Ed. Bernard Benstock. Syracuse: Syracuse University Press, 293–307.

Benstock, Shari, and Bernard Benstock. 1980. *Who's He When He's at Home.* Urbana: University of Illinois Press.

———. 1983. "*Ulysses*: Narrative Movement and Place." *Work in Progress.* Carbondale: Southern Illinois University Press, 30–46.

Benvenuto, Bice, and Roger Kennedy. 1986. *The Works of Jacques Lacan: An Introduction.* New York: St. Martin's Press.

Berberova, Nina. 1978. "A Memoir and a Comment: The 'Circle' of *Petersburg.*" *A Critical Review.* Lexington: University of Kentucky Press.

Berdyaev, Nicolas. 1962. *The Russian Idea*. Trans. R. M. French. Boston: Beacon Press.
———. 1986. "An Astral Novel: Some Thoughts on Andrei Bely's *Petersburg*." In *The Noise of Change. Russian Literature and the Critics*. Ed. Stanley Rabinowitz. Ann Arbor: Ardis, 197–204.
Berman, Marshall. 1982. *All That Is Solid Melts into Air*. New York: Simon and Schuster.
Bethea, David M. 1989. *The Shape of Apocalypse in Modern Russian Literature*. Princeton: Princeton University Press.
Bialik, Wlodzimierz. 1976. "Der Berliner Simplicissimus oder Franz Biberkopf als Exemplum in Spiel der Transzendenz" (The Berlin simpleton or Franz Biberkopf's parable in the play of transcendence). *Zagadnienia Rodzajow Literackich* 19, no. 1: 69–84.
Bidwell, Bruce, and Linda Heffer. 1981. *The Joycean Way*. Dublin: Wolfhound Press.
Biermann, Karlheinrich. 1982. "Die Lyrik der Industriemetropole: Emile Verhaeren. Mit einigen Parallelen zur belgischen Malerei im späten 19. Jahrhundert" (The poetry of the industrial metropolis: Emile Verhaeren. With some parallels with Belgian painting at the end of the nineteenth century). *Zeitschrift für Literaturwissenschaft und Linguistik* 48, no. 12: 50–68.
Blamires, Harry. 1966. *The Bloomsday Book*. London: Methuen.
Blanchard, Marc Eli. 1985. *In Search of the City*. Stanford: Anma Libri.
Blumenthal, Helene Elting. 1982. "Collaboration and Contact: City Life in *Ulysses* and *Mrs Dalloway*." Diss. University of Pennsylvania.
Bradbury, Malcolm, ed. 1976. *Modernism*. Harmondsworth, Middlesex: Penguin.
Brand, Dana. 1991. *The Spectator and the City in Nineteenth-Century American Literature*. Cambridge: Cambridge University Press.
Buck-Morss, Susan. 1986. "The Flâneur, the Sandwichman and the Whore: The Politics of Loitering." *New German Critique* 39: 99–140.
Budgen, Frank. 1937. *James Joyce and the Making of "Ulysses."* London: Grayson and Grayson.
Burkhart, Digmar. 1984. *Schwarze Kuben, Rote Dominos* (Black cubes, red dominoes). Bern: Peter Lang Verlag.
Cannon, Jo Ann. 1978. "The Image of the City in the Novels of Italo Calvino." *Modern Fiction Studies* 24, no. 1: 83–90.
Carlson, Maria. 1980. "The Ableukhov Coat of Arms." In *Andrei Bely Centenary Papers*. Ed. Boris Christa. Amsterdam: Hakkert, 157–70.
———. 1993. *"No Religion Higher than Truth." A History of the Theosophical Movement in Russia, 1875–1922*. Princeton: Princeton University Press.
Caspel, Paulus Petrus Johannes van. 1980. *Bloomers on the Liffey*. Gröningen: Rijksuniversiteit te Gröningen.
Christa, Boris, ed. 1980. *Andrei Bely Centenary Papers*. Amsterdam: Hakkert.
Churchill, Henry S. 1962. *The City is the People*. New York: W. W. Norton.
Cioran, Samuel. 1973. *The Apocalyptic Symbolism of Andrei Bely*. The Hague: Mouton.
Clark, T. J. 1985. *The Painting of Modern Life*. New York: Alfred A. Knopf.
Cooper, Margaret. 1974. "Problematic Parallels and the Ordering of Evidence in *Ulysses*

and *Berlin Alexanderplatz*: A Comparison of Analogies." *Comparative Literature in Canada* 6: 20–38.

Cope, Jackson I. 1981. *Joyce's Cities*. Baltimore: Johns Hopkins University Press.

Cornwell, Neil. 1989. "Bely and Joyce: Half a Century On." *Annali di Ca' Foscari* 28, no. 1–2: 41–48.

———. 1992. *James Joyce and the Russians*. London: Macmillan.

Crosman, Robert. 1968. "Who Was M'Intosh?" *James Joyce Quarterly* 6, no. 2: 128–36.

Doležel, Ludomil. 1979. "The Visible and the Invisible Petersburg." *Russian Literature* 7: 465–90.

Dolgopolov, L. K. 1975. "Obraz goroda v romane Andreia Belogo *Peterburg*" (The figure of the city in Andrei Bely's novel *Petersburg*). *Izvestiia akademii nauk SSSR, Seriia literatury i iazyka* 34: 47–57.

———. 1976. "Simvolika lichnykh imion v proizvedeniiakh Andreia Belogo" (The symbolism of personal names in the works of Andrei Bely). *Kul'turnoe nasledie drevnei Rus'i*. Moscow: Sovetsky pisatel'.

———. 1977. "Peterburg 'Peterburga': Gorod v romane Belogo." (The Petersburg of *Petersburg*: the city in Bely's novel). *Na rubezhe vekov*. Leningrad: Sovetsky pisatel', 266–73.

———. 1988. *Andrei Bely i ego roman "Peterburg"* (Andrei Bely and his novel *Petersburg*). Leningrad: Sovetsky pisatel'.

Dollenmayer, David B. 1980. "An Urban Montage and Its Significance in Döblin's *Berlin Alexanderplatz*." *German Quarterly* 54: 317–36.

———. 1988. *The Berlin Novels of Alfred Döblin*. Berkeley: University of California Press.

Drozda, Miroslav. 1981. "Peterburgsky grotesk Andreya Belogo" (The Petersburg grotesque of Andrei Bely). *Umjetnost rijeci* 25: 133–54.

Dudek, Louis. 1981. "*Ulysses* Comes Home: A New Interpretation." *Canadian Fiction Magazine* 40–41: 134–38.

Dumbleton, William A. 1984. *Ireland: Life and Land in Literature*. Albany: State University of New York Press.

Durrani, Osman. 1987. "The End of *Berlin Alexanderplatz*: Towards the Terminus of Döblin's Tramway." *German Life and Letters* 40, no. 2: 142–50.

Durzak, Manfred. 1979. *Der deutsche Roman der Gegenwart* (The German novel at the present time). Stuttgart: Kohlhammer.

Ellmann, Richard. 1972. *"Ulysses" on the Liffey*. New York: Oxford University Press.

———. 1982. *James Joyce*. 2d ed. New York: Oxford University Press.

Elm, Ursula. 1991. *Literatur als Lebensanschauung* (Literature as a view of life). Bielefeld: Aisthesis Verlag.

Elsworth, John. 1983. *Andrei Bely: A Critical Study of the Novels*. Cambridge: Cambridge University Press, 1983.

Fanger, Donald. 1965. *Dostoevsky and Romantic Realism: A Study of Dostoevsky in Relation to Balzac, Dickens, and Gogol*. Cambridge: Harvard University Press.

———. 1976. "The City of Russian Modernist Fiction." *Modernism*. Harmondsworth: Penguin.

Flaker, Alexander. 1976. "Roman o revolucionarnom gradu" (A novel about the revolutionary city). *Umjetnost rijeci* 20: 465–80.

Frank, Joseph. 1952. "Spatial Form in Modern Literature." *Critiques and Essays on Modern Fiction.* Ed. J. W. Aldridge. New York: Ronald Press Co.

French, Marilyn. 1976. *The Book as World.* Cambridge: Harvard University Press.

Fries, Marilyn Sibley. 1978. "The City as Metaphor for the Human Condition: Alfred Döblin's Berlin Alexanderplatz (1929)." *Modern Fiction Studies* 24, no.1: 41–64.

Fursenko, A. M. 1983. "'Tema goroda v romane A. Deblina Berlin Aleksanderplats" (The theme of the city in A. Döblin's novel, Berlin Alexanderplatz). *Vestnik Leningradskogo Universiteta* 4, no. 20 (20 October): 107–10.

Furthman-Durden, Elke C. 1986. "Hugo von Hoffmansthal and Alfred Döblin: The Confluence of Film and Literature." *Monatshefte* 78, no. 4: 443–55.

Garvey, Johanna Xandra Kathryn. 1985. "City Voyages: Consciousness and Reflexivity in the Modern Novel." Diss. University of California, Berkeley.

Girouard, Mark. 1985. *Cities and People: A Social and Architectural History.* New Haven: Yale University Press.

Göbel, Walter. 1982. "Schreckbild Stadt: Chicago im naturalistischen Roman" (The nightmarish city: Chicago in the naturalistic novel). *Zeitschrift für Literaturwissenschaft und Linguistik* 48, no. 12: 88–102.

Goldman, Arnold. 1968. *The Joyce Paradox.* Evanston: Northwestern University Press.

Gombrich, E. H. 1950. *The Story of Art.* London: The Phaidon Press.

Gorman, Herbert. 1939. *James Joyce.* New York: Farrar and Rinehart, Inc.

Grah, Drago. 1978. "Das Zeitgerüst in Döblins Roman Berlin Alexanderplatz" (The time scheme in Döblin's novel Berlin Alexanderplatz). *Acta Neophilologica* 11: 15–28.

Hardy, Florence Emily. 1928. *The Early Life of Thomas Hardy.* London: Macmillan Company.

Hart, Clive, and Leo Knuth. 1975. *A Topographical Guide to James Joyce's "Ulysses".* Colchester: A Wake Newslitter Press.

Hayman, David. 1970. *Ulysses: The Mechanics of Meaning.* Englewood Cliffs, N.J.: Prentice Hall, Inc.

Hedin, Anne. 1982. "The Syntax of Slaughter in Bely's Petersburg." *Ulbandus Review* 2, no. 2: 149–65.

Henderson, Linda D. 1983. *The Fourth Dimension and Non-Euclidian Geometry in Modern Art.* Princeton: Princeton University Press.

Herr, Cheryl. 1986. *Joyce's Anatomy of Culture.* Urbana: University of Illinois Press.

———. 1987. "Art and Life, Nature and Culture, Ulysses." In *Joyce's "Ulysses": The Larger Perspective.* Ed. Robert D. Newman and Weldon Thornton. Newark: The University of Delaware Press, 19–38.

Hessel, Franz. 1968. *Spazieren in Berlin* (Walking in Berlin). Munich: Rogner und Bernhard.

Hollington, Michael. 1977. "Dickens the Flâneur." *Dickensian* 77, no. 2: 71–87.

Holthusen, Johannes. 1973. "Petersburg als literarisches Mythos" (Petersburg as a literary myth). *Russland in Vers und Prosa*. Munich: Otto Sagner, 9–34.

———. 1979. "Andrei Bely: *Petersburg*." *Der Russische Roman* (The Russian Novel). Ed. Bodo Zelinsky. Düsseldorf: August Bagel Verlag, 265–89.

Howe, Irving. 1973. "The City in Literature." *The Critical Point: On Literature and Culture*. New York: Dell Publishers.

Hussey, Barbara Lee. 1980. "From Spatiality to Textuality: The Disappearance of the City in the Modern Novel." Diss. Purdue University.

Ivanov, Vyacheslav. 1986. "The Inspiration of Horror in Andrei Bely's *Petersburg*." In *The Noise of Change: Russian Literature and the Critics*. Ed. Stanley Rabinowitz. Ann Arbor: Ardis.

Janecek, Gerald, ed. 1978. *Andrei Bely: A Critical Review*. Lexington: University of Kentucky Press.

———. 1984. *The Look of Russian Literature: Avant-Garde Visual Experiments 1900–1930*. Princeton: Princeton University Press.

Jaye, Michael C., ed. 1981. *Literature and the Urban Experience: Essays on the City and Literature*. New Brunswick: Rutgers University Press.

Kain, Richard M. 1947. *Fabulous Voyager; James Joyce's "Ulysses."* Chicago: University of Chicago Press.

Keller, Otto. 1980. *Döblins Montageroman als Epos der Moderne* (Döblin's novel montage as the epic of modernity). Munich: Wilhelm Fink Verlag.

Kenner, Hugh. 1955. *Dublin's Joyce*. London: Chatto and Windus.

———. 1972. "Molly's Masterstroke," *James Joyce Quarterly* 10, no. 1: 19–28.

———. 1980. *Ulysses*. London: George Allen and Unwin (Publishers) Ltd.

———. 1982. "Notes Towards an Anatomy of 'Modernism.'" In *A Starchamber Query: A James Joyce Centennial Volume 1882–1982*. Ed. Edmund Epstein. London: Methuen, 3–42.

Keys, Roger J. 1983. "Andrei Bely and the Development of Russian Fiction." *Essays in Poetics* 8, no. 1: 29–52.

———. 1990. "Metafiction in Andrei Bely's Novel *Petersburg*." Manuscript of lecture given at the IV World Congress of Slavic and East European Studies at Harrogate, July 1990.

Klotz, Volker. 1969. *Die Erzählte Stadt* (The narrated city). Munich: W. Fink Verlag.

Komar, Kathleen. 1981. "Technique and Structure in Döblin's *Berlin Alexanderplatz*." *German Quarterly* 54: 318–34.

Kort, Wolfgang. 1974. *Alfred Döblin*. New York: Twayne Publishers, Inc.

Kreutzer, Leo. 1970. *Alfred Döblin: Sein Werk bis 1933* (Alfred Döblin: His Work before 1933). Stuttgart: Kohlhammer.

Kuleshova, Ekaterina. 1977. "Erotika i revoliutsiya v *Peterburge* Belogo" (Eroticism and revolution in Bely's *Petersburg*). *Russian Language Journal* 110: 77–102.

Lacan, Jacques. 1977. *Ecrits*. Trans. Alan Sheridan. New York: W. W. Norton.

Lavrov, A. V. 1975. "Andrei Bely i Grigorii Skovoroda" (Andrei Bely and Grigorii Skovoroda). *Studia Slavica* 21: 395–404.

Lehan, Richard. 1986. "Urban Signs and Urban Literature: Literary Forms and Historical Processes." *New Literary History* 18, no. 1: 99–113.
———. 1988. "Joyce's City." In *The Augmented Ninth*. Ed. Bernard Benstock. Syracuse, N.Y.: Syracuse University Press, 247–61.
Lesky, Albin. 1963. *A History of Greek Literature*. Trans. James Willis and Cornelis de Heer. New York: Thomas Y. Crowell Company.
Levy, Diane Wolfe. 1978. "City Signs Towards a Definition of Urban Literature." *Modern Fiction Studies* 24, no. 1: 65–74.
Lewis, Kathleen Burford. 1976. "The Representation of Social Space in the Novel: *Manhattan Transfer, Naked Year, Berlin Alexanderplatz.*" Diss. University of Iowa.
Links, Roland. 1980. *Alfred Döblin*. Berlin, DDR: Volkseigener Verlag, 1980.
Lodge, David. 1977. *The Modes of Modern Writing*. Ithaca: Cornell University Press.
Long, Michael. 1985. "Eliot, Pound, Joyce: Unreal City?" In *Unreal City: Urban Experience in European Literature and Art*. Ed. Edward Timms and David Kelley. Manchester: Manchester University Press, 144–57.
Lottridge, Stephen S. 1978. "Andrei Bely's *Petersburg*: The City and the Family." *Russian Literature* 6: 173–96.
Lynch, Kevin. 1960. *The Image of the City*. Cambridge, Mass: Technology Press.
Maguire, Robert A., and John E. Malmstad. 1987. "*Petersburg*." In *Andrei Bely: Spirit of Symbolism*. Ed. John E. Malmstad. Ithaca: Cornell University Press, 96–144.
Mahlendorf, Ursula. 1986. "Schelm und Verbrecher in Döblins *Berlin Alexanderplatz*" (Rascal and criminal in Döblin's *Berlin Alexanderplatz*). *Amsterdamer Beiträge zur neueren Germanistik* 20: 77–108.
Marx, Leo. 1964. *The Machine in the Garden: Technology and the Pastoral Ideal in America*. New York: Oxford University Press.
Masing-Delic, Irene. 1973. "The Mask Motif in Aleksandr Blok's Poetry." *Russian Literature* 5: 79–101.
McCarthy, Jack. 1986. *Joyce's Dublin: A Walking Guide to Ulysses*. Dublin: Wolfhound Press.
McLean, Andrew. 1973. "Joyce's *Ulysses* and Döblin's *Berlin Alexanderplatz*." *Comparative Literature* 25: 97–113.
Mercier, Vivian. 1982. "John Eglinton as Socrates: A Study of 'Scylla and Charybdis.'" *James Joyce: An International Perspective*. Eds. Bernard Benstock and Suheil Badi Bushrui. Gerrards Cross, Bucks.: Colin Smythe Ltd., 65–81.
Mierau, Fritz. 1982. "*Petersburg* oder das Ende einer Flucht" (Petersburg or the end of a line). *Sinn und Form* 34, no. 4: 801–10.
Minden, Michael. 1985. "The City in Early Cinema: *Metropolis, Berlin* and *October*." *Unreal City*. Eds. Edward Timms and David Kelley. New York: St. Martin's Press: 193–213.
Mitchell, Breon. 1971. "Joyce and Döblin at the Crossroads of *Berlin Alexanderplatz*." *Contemporary Literature* 12: 173–87.
———. 1976. *James Joyce and the German Novel, 1922–1933*. Athens: Ohio University Press.

Mochul'skyi, Konstantin. 1975. *Andrei Bely.* Paris: YMCA Press.
Muller, John P., and William J. Richardson. 1982. *Lacan and Language.* New York: International Universities Press, Inc.
Müller-Salget, Klaus. 1972. *Alfred Döblin. Werk und Entwicklung* (Alfred Döblin: work and development). Bonn: Bouvier.
Mumford, Lewis. 1961. *The City in History: Its Origins, Its Transformation, and Its Prospects.* New York: Harcourt, Brace and World.
Muschg, Walter. 1961. *Von Trakl zu Brecht: Dichter des Expressionismus* (From Trakl to Brecht: Poets of Expressionism). Munich: R. Piper.
Nichols, Prescott S. 1978. "Paris as Subjectivity in Sartre's *Roads to Freedom.*" *Modern Fiction Studies* 24, no. 1: 3–22.
Nicholson, Robert. 1988. *The "Ulysses" Guide.* London: Methuen.
Pahl, Jürgen. 1963. *Die Stadt im Aufbruch der Perspektivischen Welt* (The city in the opening of the future world). Berlin: Ullstein.
Paperny, V. M. 1983. "Andrei Bely i Gogol': Stat'ya vtoraya." *Tipologiya literaturnykh vzaimodeistvii* (Andrei Bely and Gogol: Second article. The typology of literary confluences). In *Uchyonnye zapiski tartuskogo gosudarstvennogo universiteta* 620: 85–98.
Pike, Burton. 1981. *The Image of the City in Modern Literature.* Princeton: Princeton University Press.
Piskunov, V. 1986. "O nekotorykh formakh dvizheniya v *Peterburge* Andreya Belogo" (Regarding certain forms of movement in Andrei Bely's *Petersburg*). In *Andrei Bely. Pro et Contra. Testi e studi,* 52. Milan: Edizioni Unicopoli, 141–54.
———. 1987. "Vtoroe prostranstvo romana Andreya Belogo *Peterburg*" (The second space in Andrei Bely's novel *Petersburg*). *Voprosy literatury* 10: 127–55.
Poggioli, Renato. 1960. *The Poets of Russia.* Cambridge: Harvard University Press.
Prangel, Matthias, ed. 1975. *Materialen zu Alfred Döblins "Berlin Alexanderplatz"* (Materials to Alfred Döblin's *Berlin Alexanderplatz*). Frankfurt: Suhrkampf Verlag.
Rabinaw, Paul. 1982. "Ordonnance, Discipline, Regulation: Some Reflections on Urbanism." *Humanities in Society* 5, no. 3–4: 267–78.
Reavey, George. 1951. "Le Mot et le Monde d'Andre Biely et de James Joyce" (The words and the world in Andrei Bely and James Joyce). *Roman* 2: 103–11.
Rifkin, Adrian. 1993. *Street Noises.* Manchester: Manchester University Press.
Robinson, Jeffery C. 1989. *The Walk.* Norman: University of Oklahoma Press.
Ryan, Judith. 1981. "From Futurism to 'Döblinism.'" *German Quarterly* 54: 415–26.
Scherer, Herbert. 1971. "The Individual and the Collective in Döblin's *Berlin Alexanderplatz.*" *Culture and Society in the Weimar Republic.* Manchester: Manchester University Press, 56–70.
Scherpe, Karl R. 1989. "The City as Narrator: The Modern Text in Alfred Döblin's *Berlin Alexanderplatz.* In *Modernity and the Text.* Ed. Andreas Huyssen and David Bathrick. New York: Columbia University Press, 162–79.
Schoonover, Henrietta S. 1977. *The Humorous and Grotesque Elements in Döblin's "Berlin Alexanderplatz."* Bern: Peter Lang.

Schorske, Carl E. 1980. *Fin-de-Siècle Vienna: Politics and Culture.* New York: Knopf.
Schuster, Ingrid, ed. 1980. *Zu Alfred Döblin* (On Alfred Döblin). Stuttgart: Klett.
Seidel, Michael. 1976. *Epic Geography, James Joyce's "Ulysses."* Princeton: Princeton University Press.
Sengle, F. 1973. "Wunschbild Land und Schreckbild Stadt" (Rural paradise and urban terror). *Studium Generale* 14, no. 10: 619–30.
Senn, Fritz. 1972. "Book of Many Turns." *James Joyce Quarterly* 10, no. 1: 29–46.
Sharpe, William. 1983. "Urban Theory and Critical Blight: Accommodating the Unreal City." *New Orleans Review* 10: 79–88.
Sizemore, Christine W. 1978. "The Small Cardboard Box, Conrad's *Secret Agent.*" *Modern Fiction Studies* 24, no. 1: 23–40.
Stanford, W. B. 1968. *The Ulysses Theme: A Study in the Adaptability of a Traditional Hero.* 2d ed. New York: Barnes and Noble.
Stauffacher, Werner. 1976–77. "Die Bibel als Poetisches Bezugssystem: Zu Alfred Döblins *Berlin Alexanderplatz*" (The Bible as a system of poetic references: on Alfred Döblin's *Berlin Alexanderplatz*). *Sprachkunst* 8: 35–40.
Steinberg, Ada. 1977. "On the Structure of Parody in Bely's *Petersburg.*" *Slavica Hierosolymitana* 1: 132–57.
———. 1978. "Fragmentary Prototypes in Andrei Bely's Novel *Petersburg.*" *Slavonic and East European Review* 56, no. 4: 522–45.
———. 1979. "Colour and the Embodiment of Theme in Bely's Urbanistic Novels." *Slavonic and East European Review* 57, no. 2: 187–213.
———. 1981. *Word and Music in the Novels of Andrei Bely.* London: Cambridge University Press.
Steveni, Williams Barnes. 1915. *Petrograd Past and Present.* London: Richards.
Struve, Gleb. 1959. "Andrei Bely's Experiments with Novel Technique." *Stil und Formprobleme in der Literatur: Vorträge des VII Kongresses der Internationalen Vereinigung für Moderne Sprachen und Literaturen.* Heidelberg, 458–70.
Szilard, Lena. 1967. "O strukture 'Vtoroi simfonii' Andreya Belogo" (Concerning the structure of Andrei Bely's 'Second Symphony'). *Studia Slavica* 13, no. 3–4: 311–22.
———. 1979. "Andrei Belyi i Dzhems Dzhois (K postanovke voprosa)" (Andrei Bely and James Joyce [aspects of the question]). *Studia Slavica* 25: 408–17.
———. 1983. "K voprosu ob ierarkhii semanticheskikh struktur v romane XX. veka. (*Peterburg* Andreia Belogo i *Uliss* Dzhoisa [Bely's *Petersburg* and Joyce's *Ulysses*])" (Aspects of the hierarchy of semantic structures in the novel of the twentieth century). *Hungaro-Slavica* 7: 297–313.
———. 1984. "K probleme mnogosloinykh reministsentsii" (Aspects of the problem of multi-level allusions). *Festschrift für Johannes Holthusen.* Munich: Verlag Otto Sagner, 603–23.
Takla, Daniella. 1981. "A Tale of Two Cities: A Comparison of the Role of the City in Döblin's *Berlin Alexanderplatz* and Bely's *Petersburg.*" *International Fiction Review* 8, no. 2: 129–36.
Tall, Emily. 1984. "The Joyce Centenary in the Soviet Union." *James Joyce Quarterly* 21: 107–22.

Thomas, Brook. 1982. *James Joyce's "Ulysses": A Book of Many Happy Returns.* Baton Rouge: Louisiana State University Press.
Thornton, Weldon. 1982. "The Allusive Method in *Ulysses.*" *Approaches to "Ulysses."* Eds. Bernard Benstock and Suheil Badi Bushrui. Gerrard Cross, Bucks.: Colin Smythe Ltd., 230–54.
Titche, Leon L., Jr. 1971. "Döblin and Dos Passos: Aspects of the City Novel." *Modern Fiction Studies* 18, no. 1: 126–38.
Tomei, Christine D. 1994. "'Landšafty fantazii, slyšimoj molča za slovom: Dis/Juncture as a Patterning Principle in Andrej Belyj's *Peterburg.*" *Slavic and East European Journal* 38, no. 4: 603–17.
Tsivyan, Ju. G. 1984. "K proiskhozhdeniyu nekotorykh motivov *Peterburga* Andreya Belogo" (Concerning the origin of some of the motifs in Andrei Bely's *Petersburg*). *Uchyonnye zapiski tartuskogo universiteta* 664: 106–16.
Waszink, P. M. 1988. "The Example of Belyj's *St. Petersburg.*" In *"Such Things Happen in the World": Deixis in Three Short Stories by N. V. Gogol'. Studies in Slavic Literature and Poetics* 12. Amsterdam: Rodopi, 260–65.
Weimer, David R. 1966. *The City as Metaphor.* New York: Random House.
Williams, Raymond. 1973. *The Country and the City.* New York: Oxford University Press.
Woronzoff, Alexander. 1982. *Andrei Bely's "Petersburg," James Joyce's "Ulysses" and the Symbolist Movement.* Bern: Peter Lang Verlag.
Yi-Fu Tuan. 1974. *Topophilia: A Study of Environmental Perception, Attitudes and Values.* Englewood Cliffs, NJ: Prentice Hall.
Zalubska, Cecylia. 1971. "Parallelen der Erzähltechnik in den Werken von Alfred Döblin und James Joyce" (Parallels between the narrative techniques in the works of Alfred Döblin and James Joyce). *Studia Germanica Posnaniensia* 1: 59–67.
Zamyatin, Evgeny. 1970. "Andrei Bely." In *A Soviet Heretic: Essays by Yegeny Zamyatin.* Trans. Mirra Ginsburg. Chicago: University of Chicago Press, 241–45.
Zimmermann, Ulf. 1983. "Expressionism and Döblin's *Berlin Alexanderplatz.*" In *Passion and Rebellion: The Expressionist Heritage.* Eds. Stephen E. Bronner and Douglas Kellner. New York: J. F. Bergius Publishers, 217–34.
Ziolkowski, Theodore. 1969. *Dimensions of the Modern Novel. German Texts, European Contexts.* Princeton: Princeton University Press.

Index

Addison, Joseph, 6
Aeschylus, 31, 96
Alexander I, 77
Anna (Empress), 40
Anthroposophy, 23, 24, 25
Aristophanes, 31
Aristotle, 1, 13

Badaud, 10, 16; in *Berlin Alexanderplatz*, 90; in *Petersburg*, 21; in *Ulysses*, 54, 66
Bakhtin, Mikhail, 23
Balzac, Honoré de, 4
Barnacle, Nora (Joyce's wife), 56
Baudelaire, Charles, 9
Beckett, Samuel, 47
Bely, Andrei, 16, 72, 85, 101, 104n.2; *The Baptized Chinaman*, 104n.7; "Circular Movement," 20; "The City," 43; "The Emblematics of Meaning," 25; *Four Symphonies*, 19; "Ivanov," 25; *Kotik Letaev*, 104n.7; "The Magic of Words," 23; "The Memoirs of an Eccentric," 27; *Petersburg*, 12, 14, 17, 19–46, 47, 48, 49, 50, 51, 52, 60, 63, 67, 68, 69, 70, 71, 74, 76, 77, 78, 79, 81, 82, 83, 84, 86, 87, 88, 90, 92, 94, 95, 96, 97, 98, 99, 100, 103n.1; "Sacred Colors," 28
Benjamin, Walter, 5, 11, 12, 66, 93, 105n.2; *Charles Baudelaire: A Lyric Poet in the Era of High Capitalism*, 10; *Passagen-werk*, 8
Berdyaev, Nikolai A., 35
Blok, Aleksandr: "Deception," 13;
"Hymn," 13; "The Stranger," 14; "They Ascended from the Darkness of the Cellars," 14
Bonaparte, Napoleon, 38
Boru, Brian, 73, 105n.6
Budgen, Frank, 69

Catherine II, 40
Chagall, Marc, 15
Chaucer, Geoffrey, 1
Cubism, 15
Cynics, 57

Dante Alighieri, 2
Decembrist uprising, 39
Dickens, Charles, 4; *Bleak House*, 2; *Little Dorrit*, 2; *Sketches by Boz*, 9
Diogenes, 21, 57
Disraeli, Benjamin, 3
Döblin, Alfred, 16, 101, 105n.2; *Berlin Alexanderplatz*, 14, 17, 19, 20, 21, 27, 30, 34, 52, 67, 76–98, 99
Doppelgänger, 39
Dos Passos, John R., 49; *Manhattan Transfer*, 78
Dostoevsky, Fyodor M., 19, 21, 32, 51, 103n.2; *Crime and Punishment*, 4, 10, 12, 40; *Petersburg News*, 11; *Poor People*, 4; *White Nights*, 4, 11, 12

Einstein, Albert, 72
Eliot, T. S.: "Rhapsody on a Windy Night," 14; "The Waste Land," 13

Index

Elizabeth (Empress of Russia), 40
Emmet, Robert, 72, 105n.5
Euclidian geometry, 13, 15
Euripides, 1

Falconet, Etienne-Maurice, 21, 41
Farrell, James Thomas, 49
Fischer, Samuel, 77
Flâneur, 5, 6, 7, 8, 9, 10, 11, 16, 101: in *Berlin Alexanderplatz*, 90; in *Petersburg*, 21; in *Ulysses*, 54, 66
Flaubert, Gustave, 23
Flying Dutchman, 41
Futurism, 77

Gogarty, Oliver, 104n.2
Gogol, Nikolai, 19, 35, 36, 40, 51; "Nevsky Prospect," 7, 16; "The Overcoat," 4, 16; "The Portrait," 4
Gómez de la Serna, Ramon, 44
Grimm brothers, 91

Habsburg empire, 50
Hardy, Thomas, 11
Haussmann, Baron (Georges-Eugène), 4, 31
Heine, Heinrich, 5, 8
Heym, Georg, 14
Homer, 14, 48; *The Iliad*, 59; *The Odyssey*, 51, 57, 59, 61, 64, 66, 70, 105n.4
Humperdinck, Engelbert, 91

Ivanov, Vyacheslav, 21, 25; "The Inspiration of Horror," 26, 37

Johnson, Samuel, 6
Joyce, James, 16, 85, 100, 101; *Dubliners*, 54, 55; *Finnegans Wake*, 47; *A Portrait of the Artist as a Young Man*, 17; *Stephen Hero*, 74; *Ulysses*, 14, 17, 19, 20, 21, 23, 27, 30, 34, 47–75, 76, 77, 78, 79, 81, 82, 83, 84, 87, 89, 90, 92, 94, 95, 96, 98, 99, 105n.5
Joyce, Stanislaus (brother), 48
Juvenal, 1

Kandinsky, Vasily V., 15
Kant, Immanuel, 29
Keats, John, 51
Khvostov, Dmitry I., 103n.2

Léger, Fernand, 15
Lermontov, Mikhail I., 3
London Magazine, The, 8

Moore, Thomas, 73
Murray, Josephine (Joyce's aunt), 48
Muschg, Walter, 93

Napoleon I, 38
Nelson, Lord, 53, 55
Newton, Isaac, 13
Nietzsche, Friedrich Wilhelm: *The Birth of Tragedy*, 27, 35, 38
Ni Houlihan, Kathleen, 58

Parnell, Charles Stewart, 73
Pepys, Samuel, 5
Peter I, 20, 25, 29, 30, 34, 37, 38, 39, 41, 43, 46
Petersburg myth, 19, 21, 38
Petersburg News, 11
Picasso, Pablo, 15
Poe, Edgar Allan: "The Man of the Crowd," 9, 10; "The Mask of the Red Death," 45
Positivism, 3, 15, 80
Pushkin, Aleksandr S., 19; "The Bronze Horseman," 3, 28, 29, 39, 43, 103n.2; *Evgenii Onegin*, 3; "The Queen of Spades," 4

Rambler, The, 6
Reavey, George, 47
Revolution: of 1905, 14, 20, 26, 37, 39; of October 1917, 19, 47, 100
Rhys, Jean, 16
Rilke, Rainer Maria, 12, 13
Russo-Japanese war, 42
Ruttman, Walter, 83

Shakespeare, William, 51; *Hamlet*, 57

Silver Age, 19
Skovoroda, Grigory, 21, 69
Spectator, The, 6
Steele, Richard, 6
Stendhal, Marie-Henri B., 3
Superfluous man, 3
Surrealism, 36
Swift, Jonathan, 8

Theophrastus, 6
Theosophy, 23, 24, 25, 33
Tolstoy, Lev N., 23, 51; *Anna Karenina*, 16

Turgenev, Ivan S., 3

Uspensky, Pyotr D., 15, 44

Wandering Jew, 50, 69, 70
Weaver, Harriet Shaw, 51
Woolf, Virginia, 49; *Mrs Dalloway*, 16, 19; *The Waves*, 19
Wordsworth, William, 2

Yeats, Samuel Butler, 104n.2

Zamyatin, Evgenii, 74